Been There, Read That! Stories for the Armchair Traveller

Edited by Jean Anderson

T0164529

Victoria University Press

VICTORIA UNIVERSITY PRESS
Victoria University of Wellington
PO Box 600 Wellington
vuw.ac.nz/vup

National Library of New Zealand Cataloguing-in-Publication Data

Been there, read that! : stories for the armchair traveller /
edited by Jean Anderson.
ISBN 978-0-86473-572-0
I. Anderson, Jean, 1951-
823.0108—dc 22

Printed by Astra Print, Wellington

Contents

Copyright Notices

Foreword

Suppose you travel to Spain, and walk around the Prado in Madrid. At some point you will turn a corner and find yourself face to face with Hieronymus Bosch's great triptych *The Hay Wain*. There in the large centre panel is the wagon of hay, drawn by demons and followed by the powerful—popes and kings and merchants. In fact, the wagon is being drawn from Paradise to Hell. In the left-hand panel Adam and Eve are made; and then they eat the apple and are sent from Eden. In the right-hand panel are smoke and flames and monstrous things. A giant fish head with hind legs instead of a body is swallowing a pale human figure. Cat-like creatures with insect wings lead their captives towards the darkness of a prison tower. A naked woman is being dragged across the ground; a frog sits on her genitals.

Bosch's hell-creatures can still produce nightmares. Yet the most disturbing is a small, familiar, long-beaked bird in the bottom right-hand corner. Somehow Bosch, back at the end of the fifteenth century, imagined a kiwi. His little bird ignores all the terror and destruction around it. It pokes at the ground in search of grubs—modest, inoffensive, satisfying its own small appetite.

Almost by accident *The Hay Wain* might remind New Zealanders that we have sometimes thought of the world as a big place which is best visited briefly—or even ignored while we just 'get on with things'. And it might prompt the thought that we have sometimes believed ourselves in Paradise when in fact we were in Hell.

For too long we have allowed others to report the world on our behalf. In some spheres, like politics, this happens less and less. We have embassies in India and Mexico, in Egypt and The Netherlands, in France and Russia and Korea and Japan. It would be very odd if our information about such countries were to come only through other English-speaking governments. And what goes for politics goes for the spheres of literature and culture. It is surely time to stop accepting what the marketing departments of publishers in London and New York deem interesting about other places. It is time to look at the richness of the world from our own perspectives, however muddled, and to develop our own understandings of difference—time, in other words, to make our own translations.

Not that New York and London pay much attention to the wider world in any case. 'Unbelievably, or all too believably,' writes Eliot Weinberger, 'the total number of literary translations—fiction, poetry, plays, literary essays, and so on—from all languages, published by all the presses in the United States—large, small, and university—comes to about 200 a year.'

As a reading of *Been There, Read That!* makes clear, one of the wonderful things about the literary imagination is that it can do our travelling for us. This rich collection of stories allows us to see the great variety of human experience through something like our own eyes. And we can do so without harming the physical environment we share. These may be stories for the armchair traveller, but they give us the whole world—without carbon miles. It's time we had books like this.

Bill Manhire
Director, International Institute of Modern Letters

Introduction

This project initially emerged alongside the idea of setting up a New Zealand Centre for Literary Translation at Victoria University, to provide a focal point for this important activity in this country. We also wanted to gather together people within the university who were already practising our obscure art, and to include in this network translators from the wider local and international community. Over the intervening years (four!), some of the original participants have faded away and new ones have joined, but our anthology still represents both national and international dimensions, with texts from twenty or so countries. In many cases, this is the first time the writer's work has appeared in English. Some authors are well-known within their language community, others are relative newcomers. In every case, the translator has selected his or her piece out of the desire to bring it to a wider readership and to share the unexpected pleasures of encountering a new voice.

There are quite possibly as many opinions as to what makes a good literary translation as there are literary translators. For this reason there has been no attempt made to adopt a single, uniform approach to the delicate task of making the original text speak to its new reader. Instead, you will find here translations which, to varying degrees, have retained a distinct flavour of elsewhere and otherness. Translating literary texts is a far from mechanical task, calling as it does on the translator to appreciate the nuances of meaning and the weight of the original author's choice of expression, and then to find ways of respecting these nuances and choices in the translated text. Each translation is as individual as the translator who created it; no two translators would produce the same text in response to the same original.

But the point of this introduction, and of this book, is not to dwell on the philosophical and theoretical debates surrounding literary translation. Rather, our purpose is to bring to you, the reader, the deeply pleasurable experience of being among the first in the anglophone world to listen to these voices from around the globe. We hope that you will find here something to satisfy the armchair traveller within, to excite your curiosity about a situation, a writer, a culture, and a country you may never have encountered before. To read a writer in translation is indeed to travel to a different place—bon voyage!

Jean Anderson
Director, New Zealand Centre for Literary Translation
Victoria University of Wellington

Acknowledgments

Any anthology requires the collaboration of a large number of people, and this one is no exception. I would especially like to thank the translators, local and international, who not only worked through several drafts of their texts, with me or the authors, sometimes both, but waited patiently for the project to take shape over several years. In many cases they also tracked down the rights holders for the stories and made the initial contacts.

My thanks for their support to Deborah Willis, Hansgerd Delbrück, Jim Collinge and Brian Moloughney.

Special thanks are due to Ungku Maimunah Mohd Tahir, Monika Smith, John Jamieson, and Jan Lauwereyns for their advice, and to Kyleigh Hodgson for her editorial patience and proficiency.

Andrea Grill

Andrea Grill was born in Bad Ischl in Austria in 1975. She studied Biology, Italian, Spanish and Linguistics in Salzburg, Thessaloniki and Tirana, before completing a doctorate at the University of Amsterdam on the butterflies of Sardinia. She has published two books: an anthology of humorous stories based on various members of a family, *Der gelbe Onkel. Ein Familienalbum* (Salzburg: Otto Müller Verlag, 2005), from which this story is taken, and in 2007, her first novel *Zweischritt* (Otto Müller Verlag).

My Grandmother, the Crustacean

The older my grandmother got, the younger she thought she was. When she was eighty-five she thought she was twenty-three. She drank white wine, and every afternoon at four o'clock, a cup of coffee. But neither beverage had any effect on her whatsoever. When it got dark, she always said that she had to go, that she couldn't possibly miss her bus, because she wouldn't get home otherwise. She sat there in the middle of her own kitchen, where she'd been sitting for ten long years, unmoving, and nothing on earth could convince her she was in fact at home. Her children, that is my mother and my aunt, were always saying that it was a dreadful situation, that you just couldn't talk to her any more. But you could have a pretty good conversation with her if you just accepted that she was twenty-three years old at the time.

I had wonderful conversations with her. Sometimes she thought I was her sister, sometimes my name was Renate, and sometimes I was a colleague of hers, a seamstress like her. She'd forgotten that my sewing career had ended at the age of ten after only five minutes, because I had pricked my finger, and in fact made a proper job of it because I forgot you could take your foot off the pedal under the table and stop the needle whirring endlessly up and down. I didn't have to do sewing at school any more for the rest of the year. From then on, I managed to organise my sewing so that I spent all my time drawing and cutting out patterns. My mother or sister would then sew a few seams at home before the next lesson.

At twenty-seven I broke my right ankle, just as my grandmother had broken her ankle at twenty-seven. With the difference that she jumped out of a burning house, and I, on the other hand, simply fell off my bicycle at the entrance to the university. I've often wondered, though, how high a window I could jump out of without breaking my ankle, and for a long time a house fire was one of the most terrifying things I could imagine. Devil's Mill was the name of the house my grandmother jumped out of because the neighbours on the street below called out to her that she would have to jump if she didn't want to burn to death. A few minutes later the fire brigade arrived with their net. By that time, though, my grandmother was already lying in the grass, her broken ankle raised the way she had to keep it up over the following weeks in the hospital when they hung weights on her leg so the fracture would set. The house is still there today. It's on an intersection where the railway tracks cross the street, beside the river.

Ever since I've known the house, this Mill of the Devil,

there has been a bakery on the ground floor. Later on I used to buy sweet pink biscuits there, in the shape of tiny pretzel sticks, crescents or little buns. My grandmother's leg didn't heal perfectly straight, and ever since, her ankle has warned her there's bad weather on the way. I can feel the snow tickling in my ankle too. A not entirely unpleasant sensation. They put a nice yellow plaster cast on mine, and no one would even notice today that my ankle had been broken.

I don't think my grandmother ever really got over the war. *The War*, as she called it, as though there'd only ever been one. The way no one ever really gets over any war. That was probably the reason why, when she was old and sat around in her chair all day like some sessile old crustacean, she was always very nervous when the sun went down. If she missed her bus, she wouldn't get home that evening, she would complain, come on, we have to hurry. She had to cook for her brothers, remember, and would nearly manage to pull herself up from the chair she hadn't left for months without assistance. Just the one brother, I thought to myself, because the second one had died young. Renate, she called me, squeezing my hand imploringly. I told her my name and who I was, and she smiled and told me shorter hair really suited me. In fact I had only recently had my hair cut. But it was a mystery to me how she could see that with those blue-grey eyes that were nearly blind. Normally she could barely make out anything except vague grey shapes, only recognising people by their voices. She seemed to have forgotten their faces long ago.

The older and younger she got, the smaller she became. Her face shrivelled up, and her body, which a few years earlier had still been like a soft, juicy shellfish, filling her chair although she hardly ate anything, shrank down to the size of a child that you could easily pick up from its seat and carry to bed. She no longer wanted to stay up late in the evenings. If she wasn't allowed to catch her bus, she wanted to go to bed where she would lie staring wide-eyed at nothing.

Opposite the bed was her old sewing machine, a pre-electric sewing table with moving parts operated by a foot pedal. This was the table where she once showed me how you make a knot on the end of a thread. You wind the cotton round your index finger a couple of times, roll the threads slowly several times with your thumb and then quickly pull them off your finger, making a knot. It still works, and every time I sew on a button, I first make my grandmother's knot on the end of the thread before I pull the needle through the material.

By now my young grandmother had forgotten all about knots. In her mind she had moved on to massaging the guests at the health resort. She had moved into the cellar of her house, so she could rent out the rooms in the upper storey. Summer guests, she called these people, resort guests. She enjoyed the massaging very much and she showed me how you massage people's necks. You had to hit the person's back with the sides of your hands, quickly and carefully. She often used my shoulders to show me how, and I practised on hers.

I ask if I should pour her another drop of wine. She doesn't react, doesn't make any movement that shows she has even heard me. I ask her again, then offer her a peeled orange, feed her the segments one by one, and although she doesn't tell me that she wants more, she opens her mouth willingly each time my hand approaches her face with a piece of fruit and swallows everything quietly like a well-behaved child.

I spent the first two years of my life on my grandmother's table. I lay there as she changed my nappy or fed me. Perhaps that's why I've always been particularly fond of her, and often, when I'd argued with my parents, I would glare at them and say I was going to Grandma's, I was moving to Grandma's, Grandma understood me. At Grandma's place I was allowed to stick my finger in the cake mixture, scrape the beaten egg whites out of the bowl with my whole hand, and lick the palm of my hand with relish. Beaten egg tasted wonderfully of nothing at all. I just loved beaten egg whites. At ten a.m., because in those days we got up early and were already hungry again by ten, she would cut open a bun for me and put in a whole row of milk chocolate squares. I just love buns filled with chocolate. The chocolate was so thick that you had to bite down on it really hard to get your teeth through.

At my grandmother's we never ate meat on Fridays. She always took me with her to church at Easter and always looked stern at three p.m. on Good Friday. She did the stations of the cross with me, telling me the deliciously scary story about the crucified miracle man. My grandmother taught me the bedtime prayers that I later transformed into business transactions where I did a deal with God, exchanging my good behaviour and not-fighting-with-my-sister for more interesting things, like a scooter or a special chocolate cake for my birthday. I especially liked Fridays because then we ate pastries, which already happened to be my favourite food: plum jam pastry and cottage cheese strudel, poppy seed fingers, and even pancakes filled with ice cream. It was supposed to be a punishment, to atone for the sins you had committed through the week, and to thank the miracle man who had sacrificed himself for us.

This is how I saw it at the time, but I didn't understand anything really, because for me these sweet dishes for lunch were the best treat of all. I really liked the miracle man. He stared helplessly and pathetically out from the cross with the initials I.N.R.I. engraved above his head. I read the most exciting stories in my own little Bible. About people who could walk on water, for example. A long cherished dream of mine which I have so far only managed to make come true in winter.

I can still clearly hear my grandmother's voice, calling me into the house from the garden at four p.m., when her coffee was ready and she'd made my cocoa, not just from powder but from melted chocolate. I can hear her adding a 'dear' to my name, hear her calling it 'icy cream' all the time. The older I get, the more astonished I am that I'm the spitting image of her in the photo hanging above the credenza in her bedroom. I can still hear her saying these words, forgotten words no one uses anymore: credenza, cheval glass, carver chair, sweet meats.

I would lie on her kitchen table as she cooked on a wood-fired stove that she lit in the mornings and only allowed to die down in the afternoons. Not only did she cook lunch on this stove, she also boiled up the washing there, white underclothes and sheets which, when they had boiled long enough, she would hang out to dry on the washing line between the gooseberry and redcurrant bushes. Since my grandmother stopped hanging out the washing, we haven't had many gooseberries.

My grandmother would stand in the garden and point to the north, to the patch of snow on the mountain towering above the wooden hut. Can you see her crown, the veil she's wearing, the richly embroidered dress that's so long it hides her shoes? Every year when the snowdrops and snowflakes flowered between the roots of the apple tree the Snow Queen would make her appearance too. On warm March days she seemed to like climbing onto the upper slope of the Zimnitz, looking down from there into the valley below. My grandmother also talked about the husband, the Snow King who was supposed to emerge as well from the melting snowfields. But him I never saw.

The older I get, the more my image in the mirror resembles my young grandmother's photo, hanging above the credenza in her bedroom. The older she got, the more often she remembered dark nights in dark cellars. She remembered the days when her husband returned wounded from *The Front,* which she talked about as though there'd only ever been one. He had walked over the Traunsee—along the banks of the Traunsee, she really meant, because he was no saint. That's how he got home, where he didn't actually stay but hid again, in the mountains or in the attic of the Devil's Mill, because he didn't want to go back to *The Front* because he knew it was all over anyway. The older she got, the more often she waited for the brother who'd already been dead for over sixty years.

She was a happy person, but I can't recall her voice ever ringing with laughter. When my grandmother got so old that she couldn't even be twenty-three any more, had to be even younger than that, so young in fact that she could hardly speak, she simply said she'd had enough of life. She folded her hands all the time, the way she had taught me to do on our excursions to the brightly illustrated stations of the cross, with the last picture of a pretty doll of a lad asleep under a bridal veil. Then he was meant to disappear for a few days, along with all the bells in the surrounding area, fly away and then come back on a Sunday when I was allowed to eat so many coloured eggs at my grandmother's kitchen table that I felt ill and lay down in the grass among the gooseberry bushes. Her whole life long my grandmother had folded her hands for me. And when she did, I actually did think that it helped a bit. But when I do it, it's just a way of stopping myself from fidgeting.

If it had been up to me, I would have wanted to see my grandmother sitting in the armchair in her kitchen for as long as it took me to get so old that I was already getting younger. Then we could have sat side by side in her kitchen, two old crustaceans, not going anywhere any more. But that was something she didn't want.

Translated from the German by Margaret Sutherland

Pol Hoste

Pol Hoste (Paul Gustaaf Julia Hoste) is one of Belgium's leading contemporary writers. Born in Lokeren in 1947, he graduated in Germanic philology from the University of Ghent, and began a career as a teacher of English and Dutch before moving on to journalism. He has published a dozen books and has been awarded the Cultuurprijs van de Stad Gent (1999) and the Arkprijs van het Vrije Woord (2002). This prize, created in 1951 by Herman Teirlinck, aims to counteract ideologically driven restrictions and promote freedom of expression. Hoste's work can be a challenge to the reader on several levels, as this story, first published as 'Vremde' in *High Key* (Amsterdam: Prometheus, 1995), shows. This translation was subsidised by a grant from the Flemish Literature Fund.

Outlandia

To me, the shape of each object had its own meaning. Geometry, however, decided otherwise. It categorically rejected my doodles on paper and in the sand. Let's face it: the Greeks did live centuries before me! It didn't even reckon with the line the aeroplane was tracing in the sky.

'C'est un avion, ça?' Is that a plane? Tokens of huge goodwill. *Mais moi, non.*

'C'est un dessin!' It's a drawing!

'Viens!'

At the outset: paper ruled in tiny squares. At the outset: not a crease, not a stain. The outcome: some sort of solution.

Is this how vibration, rippling, murmur, hissing, rustling, loss, preservation are put into words? *Soyez sage!*

'This measuring tape is used for measuring the body.'

'Why call it a tape measure then and not a body measure?'

'Because it looks like a tape.'

'Or because we are worms?'

'Exactly, yes. Stop being silly.' My grandmother was patience incarnate.

I travelled extensively with my parents. I've told you all about it. Maybe they sort of hoped I'd get to know other children. Or that I would find a way of making myself useful to myself. But I was adamant and watched. It was as if I only lived with my nose, or with my eyes, or with my ears. The simplest question set my mind to work. Blabbermouths had to be remarkably intelligent kids, I reckoned!

Wherever the road had been widened by digging into the side of the mountain, I put my head to the ground and looked through the fissure into the centre of the Earth. I could actually see the lava, the glistening blood of the terrestrial fireball.

While the others enjoyed a drink or photographed the view with much-too-small cameras, I studied the glistening rock flakes and crystals through my eyelashes. *High key.*

'Mais vraiment, il est un lézard.' He's a lizard.

'Ou plutôt un petit dragon.' Or a little dragon.

How can we possibly know what others are seeing or hearing? I read in books that sound and light are things we visualise by means of straight, crooked and semi-circular lines. Formulas are being devised about them, expressing the despair and dismay that take possession of the human brain when purely scientific methods are followed. See also 'progress'. In short, specialist literature used little more than plain language.

I would dance the magnetic fields of the objects and the electric charges I felt in my fingers and spine. I sang. When asked for an explanation, I told people I was singing the heat of the mountain.

'Je crois qu'il est un peu fou.' He's a bit crazy.

'Non, non, il est comme ça. Il chante la chaleur, comme il dit. On en a déjà parlé au médecin.' We've talked to the doctor. He's singing the heat, that's all.

To them, a quick dance in three-four time at some party seemed simpler. A quick waltz, a fraction, a calculated movement, nought point seven five. Enough of that.

'When I was nineteen,' the speaker said, 'I moved to this town. After which I got married. But I remained an outlander.'

'Maybe it's all in the mind,' the dancer said, retracing her steps and reading the sign her dance had written in the sand.

'I've never been able to uncover the secrets of the impenetrable houses that were built along the water centuries ago. The locals have, I'm sure of it. But I stood facing walls. Grey alpine rock cliffs are open windows in comparison.

At times my Mum and I travelled together. To France. We stayed with farmers or rented a room. I can still see her walking through the meadows with her camera and the tattered map.

She bought bread and wine for us in the villages. I still remember how she once asked for four tomatoes and the shopkeeper went and picked them in her back garden. They were hot from the sun.

"But why charge us?" I asked. "They're just growing there, no?" Funny, wasn't it?

I mean, honestly, in France conservatism is also thriving, and all the tomatoes are now grown hydroponically. Picked green, for transport reasons. Artificially ripened because of the market fluctuations. Taste replaced by advertising, flavour by suitable lighting. You didn't honestly believe the shift to the right was merely a question of political beliefs, did you?

In a hotel where we stayed, I saw a girl my age cleaning rooms. I was young, healthy and strong. I had time on my hands and struck the same pose painters occasionally do in their self-portraits. Or my mother and I walked through the landscape.

I spent the rest of the day thinking about the chambermaid. I wanted to be like her. I wanted to scrub floors, understand socialism and walk in the moonlight once a week or read a nice book. And her many worries? Those I would keep to myself.

I watched the woman wiping the butcher's counter. My mother bought the meat and I quietly pondered life amidst dead animals. I said: "See how the sun dries those tiles! The worn doorstep, a truly moving sight! Surely it must bring back memories of customers. Your mother buys pig's kidneys and calf's liver because she likes offal. And the butcher's wife cuts the meat, takes the money and leaves the rest to the maid. That's the life, boy! Why have eyes in your head if not to make you see what the world is about!"

I listened patiently to my thoughts, because I had decided to become this woman as well, to understand liberalism, cattle, traffic, the international flow of funds and the economic reasons behind so many wars. I was a lad of great enterprise. And what about the world's worries?

I probably wouldn't have the guts to charge people for my labour anyway. Funny, isn't it? Yes, I thought so. I'd move into a house in this little town, and work for my wife and the others, the way others work for me and for their wives. There will be meat and guests will sleep in cleaned rooms and love each other. I will be a cabinetmaker and make doors for the houses so that people can go inside each other's homes, and windows in the walls so that, from their rooms, people can look at the world, and coffins so that people can be buried in graveyards and returned to the Earth.'

Dancer: 'But now you live nowhere and you spend your days writing transportation documents in some harbour office, reading poetry.'

Speaker: 'So? Heavenly dew evaporates on the municipal tulips in the park. Workmen descend under the fountain and repair its noble mechanism so that passers-by can enjoy the water that is being pushed up, the splashing and the light.

I consider myself lucky not to be married to some rich family's daughter and not to be forced to start a clothes shop or a shoe shop. Plenty of surrounding villages, and challenges, on Sunday, by the moonlit ferry. And later on, being taught by her father how to do business. Trees swaying in an orchard, oil on canvas. Or a holiday in the Balearic Islands.

Mustn't grumble, though. Christian traders, my next-door neighbours, have actually stopped emptying my rubbish bin to pry into my affairs. The special police no longer stop by. I can relax now. The danger of arson too seems less acute. Nobody's taking the time to go through my rooms in my absence any more. I wonder what they found. Butter, milk and eggs? Or stale bread, smoked fish and an excellent little Holland gin?

I've no reason to complain. The gas and electricity mains are more or less where they should be in this town. The mains voltage too has hardly been stepped up these last

few years. The unsold kilowatt-hours are being channelled
into the globe, a serious anaesthetic.

How safe, compared to life in the jungle. One little
mosquito and I don't sleep a wink! Didn't you notice the
blood smears on the wallpaper? Nothing can hurt me. None
of those foreign peoples from school: the negroid type, the
Asian race, the Slavs, the Eskimos, the Mongolian warriors.
See the smears on the world, did you? Those handbooks!

Lots of Turks near the harbour. Mohammedans, the
textbook says. Apparently they come from the Middle
Ages. We do complicated exercises in Anti-Racism in year
three.

I drink coffee with a Mussulman. Unity of time and action
only. I refrain from discussing the work of Rik Wouters.
He wants to know how much money I have.

"N'aie pas peur," he says, my new friend. Don't be
afraid. "Me no fight."

"No," I say.

"Usually go like this," he says. "Someone come. Coffee?
Bam, punch you in the face."

"I had no idea," I say. My Turkish is worse than his
Dutch. He asks me where I work. I hand him the name
and the address of the haulier.

"Then, I send something," he says. I make a small incision
in my arm, not the artery. It's an old custom. My slate.

"C'est bien pour la santé," he says. Good for the
health.

"C'est très important," I say. Always bear in mind
that when we get ill and die, life is over. Blood-letting is
a tradition.

He strokes his stubble with his rough hand. The Arabs
too only write consonants. A much more accurate way of
expressing yourself. His crescent-and-sickle beard sounds
exactly the same. We're on the same wavelength.

"But," I say. "In Belgium, there is two." His Dutch is better. "Church and State." I keep mum about the liberal freethinkers' movement and anti-clericalism. I do not go into the social politics of the Radical Liberals either, the founding of the Belgian Workmen's Party, and the problems within the First International. But I do give a short historical survey of the educational system.

"Et la fraude fiscale, la prostitution, même l'avortement!" he says. Fraud, prostitution, abortion. He knows everything.

"Vous oubliez encore tout le secteur nucléaire." Don't forget the nuclear sector.

"Il n'est pas dans le Coran. Mais toute l'histoire de tous les peuples se trouve là." That's not in the Koran. But the history of every people is there.

And Clovis who accepted baptism after having had . . . knowledge of Clotilda (I could hardly bring myself to write down this biblical term, even as a child it sounded pornographic to me). (Knowledge! I did, occasionally, steal a peek at the Bible when my parents were out.)

"Nervii, Eburones, Albigenses, Frisians, Moors, Huguenots, I was made to copy their names a hundred times!" I shout. I should have become a bagpipe player, a Celt between Dover and Calais. This is Whisky. Do you copy, Alpha? The Canadians have just arrived.

Seriously. My friend wants to discuss the essence of faith. The coffee is almost cold, let's keep it short. He's an honest garage owner and he likes to discuss the Law when he's not working. A business in second-hand cars seemed in accordance with the Divine Principle.

"J'ai tous mes papiers." I got all my papers. No disrespect, but it's not as if the Prophet went on foot, is it? He rode on a donkey. *Sagen wir im heutigen Rahmen Europas mit einem Mercedes 'occasion'. These days let's say in a second-hand Mercedes.*

"The pious will be helped." (I should be so lucky.)

"C'est ça." If we all worked at a trade, nobody would be poor. Farmers must stick to their land, of course. What else? Then—for there is work to be done—I reckon we should reclaim the empty Christian places of worship, holy sites, and restore the unity of trade and faith. No, I didn't say "church and state". I said "faith and trade".

He sounds solemn now: "How many people actually grasp the meaning of life in Belgium?" He expects me to give him the answer and I answer : "C'est le matérialisme, on le trouve partout." Materialism is everywhere.

"Voilà. Et la drogue." Drugs too.

The title in my exercise book is "By fire and by sword". At the test, however, I answered "through inheritance, marriage and murder." Mistook Mohammed for Clovis. Sheer nerves. Five marks off. Confused Christ with God. Even worse. Seven marks off. Joseph and Mary with Adam and Eve, two couples though, or were they? Located Paradise in Bethlehem. Unforgivable. Tigris and Euphrates. Wouldn't you know it. The immaculate conception? Wrote "Eve". Mixed up the dove and the snake. Desperate and wayward little me called the tree of knowledge a Christmas tree. *I'm dreaming of a white Christmas.* Result: one furious teacher. And the forbidden fruit? A pine cone or what?

Note from my sweet grandmother. Dear Sir, could you kindly explain the difference between the apple as in Eve and as in William Tell? He keeps asking me, you see, since I always give him Swiss cheese for breakfast with a picture of this patriot on it. And while you're at it, dear sir, maybe you could also address the orange issue, he does know about William as in Mary but has no idea why Orangemen are orange and all, yours faithfully. My grandmother.

Snakes lay eggs, like pigeons. No problem. But despatching the prophet to Medina on a reindeer, honestly. Multiple choice. Father Christmas's Reins of Terror now? And Julius Caesar kept Goal, did he? God's name down as Joseph. Zero, and that's final. Hopeless. I had the most wonderful summer holidays with my sweet grandmother, Helena.

I never passed history first time. From the very beginning, God's own country, to the closure of the Scheldt and the separation of Church and State by Joseph, the Second of course. I did, however, confuse his Reforms with the Reformation, but managed to pass.

A quiet Sunday. Friends of my parents have come to visit. How does smoke detach itself from the glowing tip of a cigar? Surely this is much more fascinating than the difference between Gallic and Gaelic? How do the layered blue clouds float through the room on saturated air?

Starter, main course, dessert. The fragrances blend. When the men manifest the urge to make love I make myself scarce. Drinking water, spring water, holy water. Baptism may be administered in case of emergency.

I am more of an outlander than the outlanders. Take my Turkish friend. (We've ordered another coffee.) He drinks his religion, eats it and spreads its spirit. Having listened to my confusion, this sweet, patient, stubble-bearded creature wants to know if I lead a civilised existence.

"People should give as much as they take," I say, for I want to welcome him to Belgium, my country. "I suggest you take."

"You must take more than you give," he answers. "Otherwise, business no good." How could I forget! I do apologise.

"I have studied Greek, Latin, Gothic and very little Arabic. Hebrew even less."

"What makes soil fertile?" He's questioning me. I have

no idea. He volunteers the answer: "It gives more than you give."

"Exactly, it yields a good crop," I say. I am learning.

"Quick learner, you!" he says. We laugh and slap each other's backs.

"Yet," he says. "Something missing."

"You're telling me."

"I teach you," he says. We've come full circle, the essence of faith, its dissemination.

"Okay," he says. "You know fig tree? Well, why fig tree carry plenty fruit?"

Invariably nervous at orals. The tree, wait a minute! Something to do with being shy in each other's company? Or just a good year?

"Easy," he says. "It's for eating." He's right. The answer is simple, all you have to do is find it. Great wisdom.

"You still no believe in God?" he asks. I stall for time— *forwarding and stevedoring*—and want to continue to read poetry at the office. Much too serious, all this. Reading poetry.

"And the women?" I ask. The snake, the apple, knowledge and all that, some of it has obviously stuck.

"You take one look," he says. "And . . ." He checks to see if we're alone and zips his thumbnail across his throat: "You've had it." Dear, dear . . . just one look? How interesting, the confrontation with other cultures.

"Throat slashed," he says. "Understand?"

"Oui, oui, j'ai compris." I understand my friend at once. We've known each other long enough now, and need only a few words. Something tells me, for example, that it would be a bad idea to bring the Sufis into this. No, no, I won't broach the subject. We know a thing or two about keeping mum in Flanders. We're not the by-fire-and-sword type.

"I wish women did wear figs," I say in an attempt to show him the light-hearted me. But it doesn't work.

"How you live as a Christian," he asks, "if you not believe?" Hold on a minute, I think.

"I'm not engaged in any trade," I say. "Not in products, not in money. Okay? How shall I put it, on Friday we get a fresh load of fish in, which is good in connection with . . . the Ten Commandments and all, I tell myself."

"You do not trade and you live in a town!" I've blown it, I must admit.

"No," I say. "I have no faith. I'm my own outlander. Not a cow. A pig, a ram, not a sacred lamb." I don't say anything. He doesn't say anything. As I've said, a few words suffice.

"And a touch of Johann Sebastian Bach," I say, because I hate silences like this. "Unser Leben ist ein Schatten." Our life is a shadow.

"Repent," he says. "And buy yourself a *pre-owned Merc*. Diesel, dirt cheap." It'll solve my problems sharpish. He's right too. I'll be running a trade in no time. The car first.

Story number thirty-three. Remember the man with a camel and the other without? Exactly!

"You're not so young yourself," he says. Friends call a spade a spade. "Then, you grow old and have no faith, no trade, no car. And no younger wife!" I consider the matter. Such infinite wisdom.

"You stupid sod," he says, the man from Mohammedania, my worried Mussulfriend. We laugh.

I repent and come across my religion in everything. In the others, in my relatives and their relatives. I buy myself a car, a *pre-owned Merc*, and engage in trade. Diesel costs next to nothing and one fine day this young woman falls into my lap. The sheer energy! I'd forgotten about youthfulness. See! I told you!

As it turns out, however, this is just a wet dream. I tell my friend what I know about the international capital market, global food stocks and the weapon industry.

"Did you know," I say, "that when an arms plant converts to a toy factory, not one single job is lost. And that's just one example."

"You communist?" he asks.

"My Flemish family fought against other Flemish families," I say. "The same way those selfsame Flemish families fought them and Russian families. My Flemish family fought alongside Jewish families against German families. Alongside Spanish and Russian families they fought Italian and Japanese families. And all those years your Turkish family lived alongside other Turkish families on sheep rearing and prayer and the light on the mountains." That's what I said.'

Translated from the Dutch by Nadine Malfait

Maria Grønlykke

Maria Grønlykke was born in 1957. She grew up in rural Denmark, spending the latter part of her childhood in south-west Funen where this short story is set. Grønlykke graduated with a law degree in 1984 and worked in the public service until 1997. She made her debut as a writer with *Fisketyven: Historier hjemmefra* (Copenhagen: Gyldendal, 2003)—the collection of stories that includes 'A Place'—for which Bogforum awarded her its annual prize for first-time writers. She published a further collection of stories, also set in south-west Funen, in 2004 and her first novel in 2006.

A Place

It doesn't matter where. I'm certainly not saying.

No matter what. Because if anybody says where it is so that others can find it, the Jutlanders will be there like a shot. And if they turn up, it'll be ruined.

Not that you should go around bad-mouthing Jutlanders, I don't know anywhere near enough about them to do that, but if they do turn up, they'll change everything.

And not for the better, you can bet on that. That's why it's important that the Jutlanders don't hear about it.

It's the most beautiful view you can imagine.

It's the place where Johs the Redhead went for some peace and quiet the day Birgit was buried. It's a place you visit when you're feeling so desperate that life has become unbearable and you need to escape your own existence.

Or when life is full of promise, the sky is pastel blue and it seems that spring might be on its way after all. It's a place for all seasons, even though it gets rough in stormy weather. But sometimes that's just what you need. You get days like that.

It's a place that is . . . yes, I suppose you could call it unostentatious, even though that seems a bit pretentious because the word isn't used that often, but that's exactly what it is. And I suspect that's the very thing the Jutlanders don't really understand: Jutlanders don't see the grandeur in the unostentatious. That's how it seems to me anyway. They value other things.

But hold on a minute, I've already got something wrong, because in one respect this place is far from unostentatious: the incidence of four-leaf clovers in the area is incredibly high. Not just four-leaf clovers but five-, six- and seven-leaf clovers too. There are more than in any other place—and they're not even hard to find.

Just to be quite clear I want to reiterate that I'm not wanting to be rude, but there's a big difference between Jutlanders and others. Or, more to the point, there's a difference between Jutlanders and people from Funen.

A huge difference.

People from Copenhagen like to go around making fun of the trailers that country folk hitch onto the back of their cars when they're off to diddle the tax department or to pick up some cheap junk that they've bought through the *Trade and Exchange*. And I won't deny that there are quite a few of those trailers on the road. Both in Jutland and on Funen. In that respect the difference isn't at all evident.

But it quickly becomes obvious if you start looking at what's actually in the trailers. I don't mean to be unkind, but if a Jutlander drives over the bridge to Funen with a trailer full of junk, you can be almost one hundred percent certain that it'll be just as full on the way back—only this load's not junk. That's how the Jutlander manages to rip off people from Funen twice on the same trip.

And at the other end you've got some poor sods in Funen who think they've done a good deal.

Only they haven't. Not that I've ever heard, anyway.

Now, now, it's not nice to make generalisations. So I don't mean to generalise. But I don't think I'm the only person who has heard about the time a group of Jutlanders went to Funen to sell those mass-produced Madeira cakes called lemon crescents. They bought them cheap in a cut-price supermarket. Then they set up a van and a whole lot of other stuff in a rest area by the motorway just on the other side of the bridge—with balloons for the children and all sorts. They were offering free coffee, 'bottomliss cup', was what they wrote on the sign to lure people over, and it tasted terrible because they'd got it from a rest home where the wife of one of them worked and where they use instant. You just add water. It's really not fair on the residents who live there if this is all they get and they happen to like coffee. And older people often do.

Above the business about the coffee, they'd written:

'Reduced to clear: Lemon Crescents just like Mother used to make.'

As if anybody ever had a mother who baked lemon crescents. Not that I've ever heard anyway. It's not as though they were Dream Cakes or something like that. And they had them priced at five for fifty kroner. Which is a bit of a joke when you pay ten kroner apiece in the supermarket for exactly the same thing.

Nevertheless, they managed to sell the lot. Despite a bit of a slow start. People from Funen like to take their time before doing business—not like some others—and the

Jutlanders were well aware of this, so they had brought magazines and tabloids to read.

But once people had been around the trailer a few times to suss out the goods and make sure that they weren't being cheated, once they'd had a cup of coffee or two and maybe been given balloons if they had children with them, then it turned out that they could do with a decent supply of lemon crescents after all, so they bought enough to last them a while.

Those cakes keep for years.

But the worst thing was that they were also selling those biscuits you get in tins . . . Danish Butter Cookies. You could get two tins for fifty kroner because they were seconds. They'd made dents in the tins with a hammer to make them look like seconds, that's what I was told.

Although the people who said that aren't exactly well-known for telling the truth. People from Funen don't usually tell lies, but these ones do. Heaps.

So maybe it's a pack of lies, but the fact is that those tins of biscuits usually cost fifteen kroner each when they aren't seconds. When they haven't had dents made in them.

But I wouldn't be surprised if it was true, it would be typical of Jutlanders. From what I've heard.

One way or another the same thing could easily happen to that place—that unostentatious place—which is one of the most beautiful views in the whole of Denmark. It's not hard to work out that if the Jutlanders were to get hold of it, the whole place would look like an amusement park in less than a week.

That would be a terrible shame.

It's not the view from the place that's unostentatious—the view is great—it's the surroundings. For years this place has been completely undisturbed, marked only by a peaceful, humble sign bearing its name, a name nobody can remember. Yet everyone knows it's there, otherwise Johs wouldn't have gone up there that time, would he? There's really no need to make as much of a fuss about things as some people seem to think. Things can still be top-notch even if the lifestyle and leisure supplements haven't been out and slobbered all over them.

Anyway, a few years ago, it just so happened that the Queen of Denmark came driving down the road in her blue Rolls. And she drove right up to the place.

And blow me down if she couldn't tell that this was a good spot, and she had the chauffeur pull over so that she could get out and enjoy her view.

Of course it's possible that she just needed a smoke. Or a pee, maybe?

No, no, that's ridiculous. She asked the chauffeur to stop on the little grass parking area because she wanted to see the view. That's how it was. After a little while, she drove off again, she never went up to the proper place. I guess she had a tight schedule full of mayors and flags and Danes, otherwise she would probably have walked all the way up.

Up to where you can see everything. Jutland too. Or at least, some of Jutland.

It's so beautiful that most people realise silence is the only possible response.

But afterwards, after the Queen's visit, the locals really got going. I tell you! To this day there is a sign in the car park explaining how in nineteen hundred and something or other the Queen was visiting the area, saw this view and stopped her car and that is why the place is now called . . . you guessed it . . . Queen's View.

But never mind the name.

Actually, it's not even quite the right place because you have to walk further—further than she did, that is—along a track through a field with lots of different-coloured cows. Red, black, black and white and also a few Charolais I think they are. This is where all the four-, five-, six- and seven-leaf clovers are, you just have to get down and have a bit of a fossick around, then you'll see them everywhere. It's on the way up to the top and that's where the real view is.

And it is wonderful.

We're not talking about Niagara Falls. Thank goodness. I mean over there they've gone and stuck billboards up all over the place so you can hardly see the water. In fact, the way it's been done you'd think they were all Jutlanders. Including the tourists.

That's not how it is here.

That's what's so good about it.

No bus parks, no popcorn, no candy floss and hot dogs or T-shirts that lose their shape after the first wash.

Nothing but our little green islands, beautiful as can be, floating in the blue water, and above them the sky, which is usually pale blue because more often than not you decide to go up there on a fine day when you can see for miles—of course the sky was dark grey the day Johs sat up there and cried for the first time in his life, that goes without saying, it was inevitable, given the circumstances.

But most times this place is all light-blues, greens and blues—enough to make you feel like thanking God (who else?).

Over towards the west there's a whitewashed village church, the genuine article with a pediment and a red roof. It almost looks like a postcard. Or a painting. And if you look to the east there's a completely different type of church: it's a soft, pretty colour, the palest of yellows, with a black timber roof and a deep blue tower clock with gold roman numerals.

So far out in the country and so devastatingly elegant.

But the good thing is that there's still nobody selling hot dogs with crispy onion topping and no souvenir hawkers, even the conservation officials haven't made it here yet to show off with all their signs. By the way, apparently they're going to be descending on Møns Klint any day now. And then I expect that little corner of paradise with all its blue flowers will end up looking like an extension of a campground in Niagara or Jutland. But let's not worry about that now.

Because all I actually wanted to say was that there is still a little place where you can enjoy the view. And that really is something to be grateful for.

Translated from the Danish by Lisbeth Grønbæk

Christiane Rolland Hasler

Born in 1947, Christiane Rolland Hasler was initially a teacher before becoming an air hostess in order to see the world, then a librarian, to satisfy her other passion, for books. Since 1977 she has been an editorial contributor to the review *Brèves*, which specialises in short stories.

'The Surveyors' is taken from her collection *Villégiatures* (Paris: Fayard, 2000). In it she uses her trademark fantasy element to poke a little fun at French bureaucracy and people's well-known preference for staying home, 'l'esprit casanier'.

The Surveyors

'The Duite's still there!'

Down on one knee, behind the thick growth of reeds, Paul was looking at the water as if it was some kind of miracle. Beside him, Thomas was staring at it too, realising:

'It's still flowing in the same direction!'

'One less thing to worry about!' his brother sighed.

The water burbled past as if there was nothing wrong. The two men turned away.

They walked across the empty ground where a few boys, playing football, called out to them: 'Where we at today, man?' then they turned down the busy street, full of shoppers, that went up to the council offices. 'It doesn't even bother me any more!' a man in a bloodstained white apron called to them, standing in the doorway of his shop. Women carrying bread and baskets of groceries looked at them inquiringly as they passed, not daring to stop them, hoping they'd speak of their own accord, merely watching them, their eyes still full of anxiety, wafting over them like a flimsy veil. The two men said nothing. They were quite aware, all the same, of the villagers' concern, clinging to their heels like slimy drool. But since they had nothing to explain, they just waved their hands briefly: nothing to report.

'Nothing to declare, I suppose?'

The postman had stopped in front of the bank, holding a handful of envelopes, and was looking at them from under the visor of his cap, just as if they were the ones responsible. When the two men walked past without taking any notice of him, he raised his voice and pointed to the steeply sloping street: 'You're not the one has to pedal up that, eh!'

Paul barely turned his head, still walking quickly so as to keep up with Thomas, who was striding away up the hill.

'You'll have to talk to the mayor about that. We're on our way to report to him!' Then, almost shouting, because he was still moving away: 'In an hour the bulletin will be posted! Just as usual! . . . If you want to read it . . . you'll have to come back up!'

He was starting to pant, twisting his neck to look back, climbing the hill.

'At least,' Thomas said when Paul caught up, 'when they go down to the river it won't take them long to get there.'

The council offices, in a well-preserved sixteenth-century building, were in the middle of the village. When the two brothers got there they found the mayor standing on the doorstep. His forehead creased into new frown lines, he was staring at the two flights of stairs, famous for their wrought iron railing which had featured in a number of books of French baroque art. Well, that had done it, he told the two surveyors, the council building itself was affected now: there was a hairline crack zigzagging across the front steps. Their architectural heritage was affected!

'Well, there's no need to build a bridge across it just yet,' Thomas said sharply.

The mayor shrugged.

'Nothing else?' Paul asked.

'No, I don't think so,' the mayor replied, 'but this crack's got me worried. Anyway, you'll take a look too, that would be safer, and you're getting into the habit . . .'

Thomas cut in: 'So, are we going to do this report or not?' and the three men disappeared into the council offices.

While the two brothers had been surveying the village, looking for clues to its new geographical location and taking stock of any damage, the mayor had called the regional council to register his little town on the local lists and also, while he was at it, to get plenty of essential information, for example, the name of the region, the adjoining settlements, etc. And he needed all his nerve to state, in a small voice, that his village was new in the area, even though it had thousands of years of history behind it, because the secretaries weren't all that inclined to add a name to their lists, just like that, just because someone phoned them. Fortunately the mayor was used to it by now and had called during the coffee break. So the woman at the regional council hadn't argued about it, or not much anyway, just going through the motions, because she was in a hurry to join her workmates who were already exchanging the latest juicy gossip.

'This time,' the mayor told the two surveyors, 'we're in the Lot and Garonne region.'

'We'll have to get the new signs done . . .'

'And what about the postal code?'

'It's already sorted out. But the most important thing is, how did we handle it this time?'

'Pretty well!'

'It's because we're all flexible, have to be!' Thomas cackled.

The event which had just shaken, and that's the right word for it, the village of Saint-Foulx on Duite was rather strange and, you'd have to admit, unbelievable. With every downpour, the little town seemed to attract thunderstorms. Looming on the horizon, the great black rain-swollen clouds bore down on Saint Foulx, as lightning traced strange and threatening hieroglyphics across the sky. And all the while the noise, enough to shake the whole world on its foundations, made the remains of the old castle ramparts tremble, and all the crockery in the villagers' cupboards too.

The first time, the inhabitants of Saint-Foulx on Duite thought the end of the world had come. The neighbours could be seen throwing themselves into one another's arms, and brothers and sisters rushed to their elderly mothers' bedsides. The church bells began to ring all on their own. Then the whole village shook as if in the grip of an earthquake. And darkness fell.

The whole night long, groping in the dark at first and then with whatever light source they could lay their hands on, people set about making sure that everyone was safe and sound. It was only at dawn that the earliest risers noticed that there was something strange about the way the village looked. The view out over the wide plain was gone, and the trees of Toileries Wood were missing. They believed they'd come through an unprecedented catastrophe. They thought they'd at least survived a huge tide that had suddenly swelled the waters of the Duite. It was only when a few of the old folk—heading for the first mass or the first beer—turned into the square where the council offices were, along with the church and the Old Post Office Café, that reality smacked them in the face: no getting away from it, Rue des Tisserands was flat! Madame Tramons, who was first to arrive on the scene, had stopped short, unable to believe her eyes. She knew damned well that to get to the church she generally had to slow down at the bottom of the street and save her strength for the steep climb up to the centre of the village. But on this particular morning, here in front of her was Rue des Tisserands . . . completely flat . . . with the church porch over there at the end of the street, right in front of her, on the same level!

And that wasn't the last of the surprises in wait for Saint-Foulx. The whole village was as flat as a pancake! If you were to believe the historians, Saint-Foulx on Duite, founded many centuries earlier, had always occupied a hillock above the wide plain of Essarts, but now the hill had disintegrated and the village had been flattened out.

Except it wasn't quite as simple as that. The village had indeed been flattened out, and did its best to get used to its new state. But it wasn't on the same plain. No, this was more of a valley stretching away to the north and the south, while in the east and west the ground began to rise, reaching up to form the rocky walls visible in the distance. Saint-Foulx had simply been dropped there, smack in the middle of the valley, blocking it.

The mayor had quite a lot of bother with the railway services and the Ministry of Transport and Roads. These gentlemen wanted to know why on earth the residents of Saint-Foulx had taken it into their heads to set up their village here, cutting off the road and the railway! As if there wasn't plenty of room somewhere else! And first and foremost, did they have authorisation? By what right had they come and plonked themselves down there? Thomas had calmly replied that it was nothing to do with the villagers, and that anyway their village wasn't a flying carpet.

The mayor—and this made everyone realise that it was no accident he held this position of authority—managed to get all these agitated people to calm down a bit. He assured the relevant public services that he would definitely have the village declared a disaster zone and that the insurance companies would then take responsibility for building a detour for both the road and the railway. People's anxieties eased, and the regional council chairman signed the official declaration that the area was a disaster zone without really reading the files or going into what looked to him, at first sight, to be complete craziness—he had other fish to fry and after all, whenever there was a detour constructed there was an official opening, as well as several more kilometres of roading to add to his region's statistics. And that was it as far as this strange story went, about a village turning up one fine morning, holus bolus, with its houses and its inhabitants, its little gardens, its church and its ruins, its remnants of ramparts, the school and its three chestnut trees. A complete village, with even its river, still burbling away on the other side of the waste ground.

So the mayor decided not to alert the press, or the soil specialists or the hovercraft designers. The high school students were enrolled in the nearest schools, which didn't make the classes overcrowded. The extended family members who came to visit as usual during the holidays, older children studying at university or relatives who'd moved away to work in the cities, were a bit surprised to find the trip was shorter or longer depending on where they were coming from, but they were all delighted to see that there was now a railway station right in the village. The new Saint-Foulx station didn't appear on any timetable, but the trains had simply begun to pull in there, since there was a station building and a man in a cap waving a red flag. The mayor was quick to send off the taxes to the appropriate authorities so as not to attract attention, and life returned to its usual state of dullness.

But not for long. The storms had started early that year. With the very first one that blew in from the east, so noisy it was as if the mountain itself was collapsing, Saint-Foulx was shaken again. The villagers went crazy when the chandeliers began to swing from the ceilings. And they just had to face facts: the village had taken off again, out of the valley.

Ever since, travellers are always surprised at the way the road swerves, for no apparent reason, in this deserted area.

And so, storm by storm, Saint-Foulx on Duite travelled around, lock, stock and barrel. Accusations and threats poured into the mayor's office. The town councillors had endless meetings and eventually offered to resign: no one put their hand up to replace them. But everyone was in agreement on one point: they would deal with it among themselves. No way were they going to call in the experts: that would be far too expensive, that was the one thing you could be sure of.

Paul and Thomas weren't originally from Saint-Foulx. They'd turned up in the village one fine morning, unshaven and carrying enormous backpacks. To earn a crust, they'd tried to find work, and over the summer they'd tinkered away here and there, working as labourers on various jobs, mostly gardening. In the end the mayor had taken them on for the upkeep of the public green spaces: a little tree-lined walk with the village monument to the fallen of the Great War, the waste ground cum football field, and the few flower beds in front of the council offices. They were also in charge of keeping the streets clean and in good order. They were known as the roadmenders.

When the village began to travel about, their workload increased. They were called on to survey Saint-Foulx, to take note of its new location, any new slopes, and damages too.

Whether the village had set down on flat land or on the side of a hill, the ground suffered from such mistreatment, since although it did its best to adapt it hadn't been designed for such upheavals. The strangest thing of all was that the well at the bottom of old lady Tramons's orchard was never dry.

The two brothers soon worked out a special code that allowed them to indicate on a map, through a system of arrows and other symbols, the new layout of the streets. Then they passed this on to the mayor, and he gave all the useful information to his residents.

It sometimes happened that some of the houses found themselves on a slant, looking like the tower of Pisa; their stairs would be practically unusable. For some bizarre reason, the little gardens in the village did pretty well; no erosion, no uprooted trees. Respecting their plantings, the vegetable gardens never lost so much as a leek or a cabbage in all the disturbances. That was some comfort, after all.

But you can't travel without hitting an occasional snag. Whenever the village settled, there was some risk. The first thing to go was a tree: the acacia in Dr Lefileur's big garden was reported missing in action after the arrival in Provence. Then a few acres of land went: a bed of irises and the old stone wall, a section of the hawthorn hedge on the side nearest the Rouet farm. Or even part of a walking track: this particular loss wasn't considered very important because it led to the Toileries Wood, which was pretty far away these days.

New proverbs, previously unknown, were on everyone's lips: 'A village that travels . . . soon unravels!' The older folk thought long and hard, clinging obstinately to the edge of their empty memories, as if pieces of them were about to crumble away as Saint-Foulx moved about.

Little by little the cracks noted by the roadmenders turned into gaping holes and the losses increased. When the ruins

of the old castle disappeared during one transplanting, the
villagers were saddened. They'd always been there, those old
stones, always been just the same. But Thomas laughed at
them: oh come on, a bunch of old stones! It's true the site
was dangerous and maintaining it had always taken too
big a bite out of the village budget. Good riddance!

The next move, just as brutal and unforeseen as the
previous ones, took Saint-Foulx to the Savoie region. The
village landed, completely skew-whiff, on the rocky slope
of a towering mountain. There was the most dreadful fuss!
The two brothers were the first to notice, in the morning,
that Dr Lefileur's property had disappeared. Saint-Foulx
had once again lost a piece of itself en route. Saint-Foulx
no longer had a doctor. 'Here,' Thomas said, 'the air is
clean. You won't ever be ill.' The villagers took comfort in
the realisation, a little late, that the good doctor had had
a tendency to take unfair advantage of his monopoly. The
old ladies, deprived of the doctor's waiting room, got into
the habit of sitting in the sun on the banks of the Duite,
looking out over the stunning landscape that it took them
a long time to get used to. And the river was so terribly
noisy now! The sweet, faithful Duite had turned into a
raging torrent. It swept along, joyous, voluble, frothing
up masses of foam.

Depending on the terrain, the Duite sometimes reversed its
direction. 'Which means,' Thomas remarked, 'that the same
water can flow under the same bridge several times.'

As the months went by, the village seemed to be seized
by a kind of restlessness. It stayed in the same place for
shorter and shorter periods. Hardly had it settled, hardly
had the map of its new location been carefully drawn up by
the two surveyors, than Saint-Foulx began to shake again,
and look out, lads! Each time, some new chunk was lost.
It was making the villagers feel quite dizzy.

Where in the beginning they'd been suspicious, watchful, not quite knowing what to think about it all, now it seemed as if a great weariness had set in. Not to mention that some families had been broken up. For example, the mayor's cousins, on his mother's side, hadn't made it to the Dordogne. Paul and Thomas had informed their boss that their little house hadn't made it, or their orchard.

The ones who were left didn't know how these losses came about; they simply noted them, or criticised them. Did they happen voluntarily? And if so, how did people do it? In any case, there was no news of the missing: since they didn't know where the village had gone to, how could they have made contact again?

Despair and then anger gradually ate away at Saint-Foulx on Duite.

And then old lady Tramons lost her cat and never got over it. She kept on looking for it. Every time the village moved again her mind was a little more affected. Children laughed at her and she would threaten them: 'Just you wait and see! It'll be your turn one day! You'll drop down into hell next time we move!'

The two surveyor brothers realised things had come to a head the morning they found the villagers gathered in the square in little groups, not going home. 'Everything's fine,' the mayor had once again affirmed, 'the situation's under control!' The administrative questions had been dealt with quite quickly; practice makes perfect. Everyone would soon get a look at the map and be given a copy. The new signs would go up shortly. And, as usual, they would make sure the village didn't attract attention.

Nevertheless, along with the mayor, the two surveyors could see the villagers were growing more exasperated. Instead of resigning themselves to it, they wanted it to stop, wanted the councillors to take action, find a solution, do whatever was necessary; otherwise what had they been elected for? People got together to complain about everything. The discussions escalated. The boldest were starting to speak out. This wasn't a nomad village! Their houses weren't tents! They wanted to be settled. Maybe not to go back to where they started from, they were prepared to be reasonable, to make an effort; but they should stay here at least. They could put down nice strong roots here. The world should go back to turning normally, the village would be tucked away, in one place, it didn't matter where, as long as it was stable and not uprooted again.'We should just use an anchor!' yapped some young lad who'd served in the Navy.

But it was no use talking about ropes and ties and steel cables, they couldn't rein in their fear. It spread everywhere, penetrating every household, wafting from one end of Saint-Foulx to the other, like a bad smell.

In the old days . . . At this point in the discussion, everyone turned to the two brothers: they didn't know much about the old days, these two, who weren't actually from here . . .

Although they'd been in Saint-Foulx for several months, Paul and Thomas still kept their backpacks hanging in the hallway of their home, a furnished flat provided by the mayor's office.

Where were they from anyway? No one had ever shown any interest in this at the time when their labours had been useful. No one had asked them any questions.

Soon people began to blame the two strangers.

And that's when Saint-Foulx, practically cut in half, found itself on the seashore. Fascinated, the villagers watched the waves licking at their walls. They implored Fate to let them stop travelling about, to let this be their journey's end. Over the moon, the children deserted their bit of waste ground, with the Duite still clinging to it, in favour of the beach.

This time, everyone insisted on the one condition that seemed essential to put an end to this madness. Paul and Thomas must leave as soon as possible. The mayor tried hard to defend them, but how can you talk sense to people who don't know which way is up?

The two surveyors buckled up their backpacks. They set off on foot, towards the end of the afternoon. There was no one standing in their doorway to see them off. They had soon left Saint-Foulx on Sea. For a while they walked along beside the water, then they turned inland to climb a dune. And there, finally, they turned around. They could see the whole village spread out in front of them. Paul and Thomas sat down and took out some food. In the distance the light was fading. In Saint-Foulx people were going home, closing the shutters for the night. Then, as dusk fell, the tide began to come in. Up on their dune, the brothers ate unhurriedly, watching the show. The entire ocean was moving towards Saint-Foulx, panting as it came. Little by little, the water was gaining ground. The Duite gurgled as it hurried to the sea; it didn't have far to go to reach its goal.

The two brothers saw the church spire sway for a few moments against the setting sun, like a compass needle.

'It's still rolling like an old rowboat! I hope they've got their sea legs,' Thomas muttered.

'What a great way to go!' murmured Paul, while Thomas unfolded his map, and with a glint in his eye, started planning where to go the next day.

Translated from the French by Jean Anderson

Franz Xaver Kroetz

Franz Xaver Kroetz (born in Munich, 1947) is well-known in Germany, both as the country's most produced living playwright, and as an actor in a *Dynasty*-style television soap opera, a role which made him a media superstar. His first major success was the 1978 play, *Mensch Meier*, a family drama which is fairly representative of his early, 'super-realist' style.

This story, 'Umzug nach Berlin', is taken from a collection entitled *Blut und Bier: 15 ungewaschene stories* (Blood and Beer: 15 Unwashed Stories), published by Rotbuch Verlag (Hamburg) in 2006.

Moving to Berlin

'The wild side,' he said, sipping his red wine, 'that's what it's all about. You've got to walk on the wild side. Then you can be an artist, then you can write!'

She nodded. She was tired. She was struggling not to fall asleep. If only he would let her get a word in edgeways every once in a while, then it would be easier to stay awake. But she was to be the listener. Those were the rules, that was the game.

'But how can you get there? Back to those stories, the way I used to rip through them back in the old days, when we were in Bali.'

'In 1781,' she said, because she wanted to get in quickly.

'Don't you mean 1971?' he said and looked at her, the

way you look at a dog that's been run over by a car, still alive, but not worth calling the vet for.

She nodded.

'I used to just rip through them, seven closely typed pages, 66 lines of 75 characters including spaces, the whole page chock-full, left to right, whacking them out, spitting them out, spewing them out. Like in Bali, or wherever, back in the old days, that feeling of being one with the text, creating itself as you punch it into the typewriter, the speed of the letters multiplying on the portable typewriter!'

'Yes,' she said. 'Yes.'

'Oh God,' he said happily, 'Writing on a high, sure it was an artificial high, you can always help it along a bit, but sailing away on the ferry Ecstasy to the wild side! And that was where you'd find that mix of chaos, hard work, despair, manic energy, hysteria and courage! Courage and strength!'

He stretched, nearly made it to his feet, flopped back into the leather armchair.

She thought the monologue must be over, since he'd stopped speaking, and said: 'Shall we go and brush our teeth?'

He stiffened, glared at her through slitted eyes and said: 'That's it! Anxiety. If you're anxious, you can't get to the wild side any more. They don't sell tickets to anxious travellers.'

She didn't get it.

'It's really quite simple. When I was twenty, or twenty-one, I had three of my teeth pulled out by a dentist—all at once, all in one go! Teeth that showed, teeth I needed. The dentist told me: "You can't afford to have them fixed, it's too expensive, we'll extract them and you can stop worrying about them, and when your career takes off you can have a bridge made."'

'Of course that's hard for a young man,' she said.

'No it's not,' he shouted, getting worked up, 'no it's not! I didn't give a stuff. Oh God,' he exclaimed, maudlin, 'I lost three teeth and I didn't give a blind rat's ass. I wasn't anxious! I wasn't anxious at all. When I was young I didn't know what being anxious was. Everything,' he said, going red in the face, 'everything was so completely full-on, anyway, everything was so existential, if you like, yes, I was so existential, I wasn't anxious about a gap in my teeth, or bridgework or dentures!'

She remembered the full plate dental prosthesis that had cost him 34,000 Marks, and his health insurance had only covered twenty-five percent.

'Look how depressed I was last year,' he said, shaking his head, 'when I got that hideously expensive full plate, that I didn't need at all, really.'

'What do I need, after all?' he asked, full of emotion, looking round. 'A new Duden dictionary, some paper, my old portable typewriter and a few ideas that are worth having a whack at. Oh, God.'

He stood up and then fell to his knees, moaning. 'That's not really so much to ask of you, is it, to give this old man what I need: I want my old portable typewriter back, the one I wrote "Helga Is No Dog" on, in Bali, where is it?'

His wife realised this was no time to say, 'I don't know.' To calm him down, this crisis couldn't last forever, she said, 'I think it's in the basement, love. Don't worry, I'll find it for you tomorrow.'

'I want my old portable typewriter, I want a hundred sheets of blank paper, 80 gsm weight, I want a dictionary with the new reformed spellings and I want an idea!'

'I'll buy you the paper tomorrow and the new Duden,' she said, 'You've . . .'

'I've made a lot of mistakes,' he said, gazing at her earnestly, 'and you, you've completely ruined me,' he added, looking at his 35,000-Mark computer. 'You and the full plate, you've been the ruin of me. From tomorrow on I'll be writing without the plate and without the computer. After all, Zen monks aren't even allowed to wear dentures. By your gaps shall you know yourself! And I want a monthly bus pass again, too, same as in the old days. We'll deregister the Jag.'

'Yes, darling,' she said, 'I can do all that tomorrow, no problem at all.'

He looked around.

'Oh God,' he said, 'nobody can write surrounded by all this goddamned wealth!'

Their villa in Obermenzing was still mortgaged to the tune of half a million, but the property was worth three times that amount.

'I can do something about that tomorrow,' she said, a bit more cautiously.

'I don't want you to do something about it tomorrow, I want you to sort it out right this minute!'

'I'll call the paper tomorrow and find out what their deadline is for the weekend property section.'

'I want to go back to our old flat in Pasing, next to the railway station.'

'I'm afraid the house has been demolished, darling.'

'Then I want some other cheap pad. We'll move to Berlin,' he said, beaming. 'A completely new start, no Jag, no plate, no computer, no bloody villa, somewhere in Kreuzberg, some old place. There's any number of old derelict buildings in Berlin.'

He was crowing with delight: 'We'll move into a Plattenbau! No car, no computer, no teeth, no anxiety!'

'We'll do that, darling, first thing tomorrow. That's no problem, by the time you get up, I'll have most of it sorted—don't get anxious!'

He humphed, he swallowed, he was having trouble breathing, she was getting worried.

'And I'll start smoking again,' he exclaimed, 'I'm going to smoke again the way I used to. I used to smoke Rothändle, unfiltered, later with filter tips, but always Rothändle. I want Rothändle unfiltered.'

'That's not a problem,' she said. 'There'll be some on your breakfast tray next to the morning paper.'

'I don't want a breakfast tray. I never had one back in the old days, I want to get up, the same as everyone else, black coffee, Rothändle, and attack the typewriter.'

'Not a problem, darling,' she said. 'I can sort all that out and get it done for you tomorrow. You can count on me.'

He looked into his wine glass, then at the bottle.

'And I don't want this bloody Italian wine at forty Marks a bottle any more. Back in the old days, I drank vodka!'

She was frightened but didn't let it show. It was just that she was worried about his health, and if he really was going to start tomorrow on the Rothändle and vodka, things could get tricky.

'One of those cheap brands, Pushkin or Ivan Rebroff or whatever.'

'Yes,' she said, making up her mind not to buy any vodka.

He smiled.

'Rebroff! That's that fat Russian singer, before he turned into a fat Russian operetta singer in Augsburg, he used to sing Russian songs better than anyone. So tenderly, so beautifully, so . . . I used to listen to Rebroff's Russian songs all night long. And I wrote. Can you . . .'

'That might take a while, I'll have to check out a couple of second-hand shops that sell old records, but I'll get them for you, darling, Ivan Rebroff, Russian songs . . .'

'Recorded around 1965, that's important, because maybe he's re-recorded them and I don't want that.'

'Of course, darling, don't get excited, that's what a wife is for, isn't it?'

He nodded, wheezed, poured the rest of the wine into the glass, drank and said, hesitantly, almost shyly: 'You do understand me? There must be some reason why I'm not writing any more, why I just can't put a sentence together, why . . . I'd be happy with crap, but I can't even come up with crap, I can't come up with anything any more. The faster the computer, the less I come up with.'

He began to cry.

'I love you,' he mumbled, 'but we decided not to have children, because I wanted to write, because I'm a writer.'

'Yes,' she said, thinking she would have liked to have his child.

'I'm your little boy, that's what I always said, right?'

She nodded. 'Go and brush your teeth now?'

He dragged the 34,000-Mark full plate out of his mouth and yelled, 'Are you doing that on purpose?'

'For goodness' sake, don't,' she shouted. 'Remember how angry you were when your health insurance would only pay twenty-five percent.'

He stared at the plate, and smiled, and she saw the glint of the sharp golden stumps it had been anchored to. Now he looks like a rabid golden rabbit, she thought and hoped that he wouldn't be able to read her mind.

'This thing,' he said less firmly, gripping the plate tightly, 'this thing is going into the rubbish bin, right now.'

Weaving unsteadily on his spindly legs he made his way to the kitchen, and she heard the bin lid clatter open, clatter shut.

He came back.

'And now I'm going to bed, without brushing, because I have no teeth left worth the effort.' He seemed happy.

'Yes darling,' she said, 'that was a blow for liberty, wow! I'd like to see anyone else do that!'

'Yes,' he said sarcastically, 'I'd like to see Handke or Botho Strauß throwing away their teeth! From now on you're only going to see me with no teeth.'

'Bravo,' she whispered, and kissed his hands.

'With these hands I shall return tomorrow to the honest hard labour of the writer, to my old portable typewriter, to the blank sheet, and I shall write, write, write!'

She nodded and got up: now, finally, they were going to bed.

He fell asleep at once, she lay awake. She was thinking about tomorrow, and somehow she was looking forward to it. Perhaps it really did mean starting a new life at long last, a pared-back new life. She wasn't that enamoured of the old one anyway, and she thought she might quite like to move to Berlin. Then she fell asleep too.

When she woke up he was already out of bed. She went looking for him. He was sitting at his computer and said: 'Don't bother me.'

She went into the kitchen and put on the kettle for a cup of tea. Then she remembered and opened the rubbish bin. She rummaged all through it. She couldn't find the full plate.

She went to his room and asked whether he wanted a cup of tea as well.

He said, 'Why are you asking me this stupid question, I've been drinking coffee for the last thirty years, or haven't you noticed?'

Light glinted off his teeth, a full set of choppers.

Translated from the German by Monika Smith

Axel Hacke

Axel Hacke was born in Braunschweig in 1956, and studied in Göttingen and Munich. From 1981 until 2000 he worked as a sports journalist and later as a political reporter for the *Süddeutsche Zeitung*. He is the author of over a dozen books, and has been awarded the Joseph Roth Prize, the Theodor Wolff Prize, and the Egon Erwin Kisch Prize (twice). His work has been translated into several languages.

Waste

Where in other countries you may struggle to find a single rubbish bin, our beloved Germany offers no fewer than four at once. And in many houses there's even a special room for sorting rubbish—with bins for compost and yoghurt lids, preserving jars and paper, plastic and batteries, glass and wood, surplus pharmaceuticals and chemicals, and of course a bin for the small amount of leftover rubbish that defies classification. This used to be the 'hobby room'. Then there are those empty bottles with the refundable deposit, they're stored here too, along with empty cans—don't forget the cans!

These rooms have been known to become rather cramped.

But the introduction of car bumper deposits has brought some Germans to the edge of despair.

Not so long ago, whenever they got a small scratch on

their bumpers, for example while parking (Germans are sensitive about such things), they simply went to the nearest car bumper shop or the car bumper section at the Karstadt department store and bought a new one. The old one went in the rubbish.

But then the Car Bumper Recycling Act of 1999 made this illegal. Bumpers now had to be thrown into one of the country's many scrap metal bins.

Unfortunately, it turned out that the existing scrap metal bins were generally too small for this purpose.

So the federal government passed the First Implementation Regulation of 2000 Concerning the Car Bumper Recycling Act of 1999, which required the installation of devices known as car bumper shredders alongside scrap metal bins nationwide. Bumpers thrown into the shredders would be chopped into small pieces. However, a resident of the North German town of Neumünster considered this regulation to be in breach of noise pollution laws. He has instituted legal proceedings. The enquiry is still in progress, and a decision is not expected before the year 2013.

To deal with the problem in the meantime, numerous regional governments then decided to introduce so-called Car Bumper Recycling Transitional Regulations, which would see scrap bumper containers installed on every second street corner. Two measures were meant to keep the noise problem under control. First, the containers were to be padded with old tyres on the inside, and second, they would be able to contain only one bumper at a time to avoid unwanted clattering.

However, the installation of these scrap bumper containers was met by protests from the citizens' initiative 'Beautify Our Neighbourhood' with mass demonstrations in all regional capitals. As regional parliamentary elections were approaching in several of the regions concerned, the implementation of the recently approved Car Bumper Recycling Transitional Regulations was put on hold. Furthermore, as many people hadn't got rid of their old bumpers anyway, but were storing them at home until the matter was clarified, it would have been impossible for the scrap bumper container manufacturers to produce sufficient scrap bumper containers, considering that the Implementation Provisions of the Car Bumper Recycling Transitional Regulations required the new scrap bumper containers to be made from scrap bumpers. But as there was a shortage of scrap bumpers, the containers could not be built.

Meanwhile, the rubbish-sorting rooms of many German households had started to look a complete shambles. People began to grumble. Many German children had to sleep in their parents' beds because their own rooms were needed as storage space for scrap bumpers that had been tarnished, scratched, dented slightly or otherwise damaged.

For this reason, many local governments moved to introduce inner-city car bumper deposit systems. All specialist car bumper retailers would be required to take back any car bumpers they had sold and refund a coin paid as a deposit. Legal challenges came from both the Federal Association of Car Bumper Retailers and the South German Car Bumper Users' Club. In any case, the regulations proved to be unworkable, as many Germans buy spare bumpers during their lengthy journeys through Germany and other countries, so what is really needed is a nationwide scrap bumper return system, but this will become feasible only once the legal problems outlined above have been resolved.

Just recently the EU Commissioner for Coloured and White Metals has announced the introduction of a regulation for the whole of Europe.

But for the many Germans whose houses are overflowing with scrap bumpers, the situation is fast approaching crisis point.

Translated from the German by Richard Millington

Partow Nooriala

Partow Nooriala was born in Teheran in 1946, and started writing classical poetry at the age of thirteen. Her first book, *A Share of the Years*, was ready for distribution in 1972, but was banned until the Pahlavi regime was overthrown in 1979. In 1986 she moved to the United States. She is the author of *Of the Eye of the Wind, My Earth Altered, With Chained Hands in this House of Fortune, Like Me*, and *Mihan's Future*. None of her poetry has been published in Iran again.

This story is taken from a collection entitled *Like Me*, published in Persian by Pars Books and Publishing in Los Angeles (2003).

Se-pa-ra-tion

Shamsi and Kazim separated. Shamsi and Kazim sepa-separated. Se-pa-ra-ted. Father and Mother separated. The day of the eclipse of the sun, the day when they were taking my brother and me to Grandfather's house, Shamsi and Kazim separated. At the same moment Grandmother clutched her silver hair and shouted in Grandfather's deaf ear: 'Shamsi and Kazim separated,' my father and mother separated. I ran to my childhood cradle in which my brother was now sleeping and shouted at the top of my lungs, 'Shamsi and Kazim separated.' My brother woke up with a start and began to scream and my mother, tears streaming down her face, stood up from the corner of the room and took my brother into her arms then began stroking my head which she had clutched and pulled into her skirt. Separation, se-pa-ra-tion. With my fingers strand by strand I separate my brother's curls so they lie separated, and I pull a handful of his hair away from the large lump on his neck and clutch the lump to separate it from him. Mother says, 'My baby's neck is crooked.' Then she says, 'My heart grows heavy when he looks at me,' and she separates my fingers from his separated curls. Grandmother separates her hands from the stair railings, waves them in the air, and moans, 'What your hands sow, your children reap.' My mother separates my brother from my childhood cradle and tearfully says, 'Oh Mother, please stop. What has this innocent child done to have to pay for Kazim's sins?' Mother sits down still holding my sleeping brother who's now sucking on his dummy, and puts him on a blanket she has spread on the floor. I sit next to her so I'm not separated from her. I lay my head on her lap. She says, 'I'd die for you,' then with her fingers she separates the curls on my head. The day darkens behind my heavy eyelids and everything around us becomes black and white. Only the beads on the pendant round Shamsi's neck keep their colour. My mother laughs and presses my curls together and presses me to her breast. Then she presses one hand to my brother's soft neck which is free of the lump, and the other to her necklace, pressing the beads together so they are tightly bound. But the string breaks and the beads separate, fall and scatter separated on the floor. We and everything around us are bathed in colour, but Grandmother's hair is still silver and Grandfather's ears are still deaf.

Translated from the Persian by Sholeh Wolpé

Breandán Ó Doibhlin

Breandán Ó Doibhlin is a leading writer, critic and translator in Modern Irish. Born in Rooskey, Co. Tyrone (Northern Ireland) in 1931, he studied at St. Patrick's College Maynooth and in Rome. He was appointed Professor of French in 1958 and went on to become a major influence on the development of modern criticism in the Irish language. His most valuable contribution to writing in Modern Irish is however his development of a wholly distinctive and original voice for modern Irish prose writers who had become hostage to the nationalist pieties of social realism. In two major novels, *Néal Maidne agus Tine Oíche* (1964) and *An Branar gan Cur* (1979), Ó Doibhlin experimented with characterisation and narrative, fusing elements from indigenous writing with innovative approaches from other traditions. *Néal Maidne agus Tine Oíche* (Morning Cloud and Evening Fire) is a fable telling of journeys, dispossession, loss, and a voyage to a promised land which proves to be less than ideal. It details the trauma that results from cultural and linguistic dispossession and, echoing biblical and mythological themes, explores the necessary if fraught relationship between speaker, language and place.

The Poison Within

This is how the able father would begin his story:

Know you that we were always under the spell of the ocean, that we always felt the summons to go out across the eternal seas. We were only ever happy watching the furrows ploughed by our ships on their shining surface.

What drew us always was the longing for home, a home that we never knew but which did not stop us nevertheless from always hankering after it. We did not know what kind of land this was to the west that was calling out to us across the bright waters. But a blessed island appeared to us way out to sea where the sun sets, a land of grassy plains and innumerable, bright strands. Not a rich land but one that would sustain a hardy race of men. And through all our misfortunes we never lost the obscure hope of finding that kingdom, the kingdom of liberty where we would decide on our own destiny and where we would sing the songs of the ancients forever in our own tongue. For I know of no sweeter music nor greater source of strength than the longing for a place to stand.

We spent years building our ships, working amidst the smell of wood and pitch, the noise of hammers and saws, nailing and caulking, corking and rigging. And I used to listen to the songs of the workers and it was sweet to hear the longing for the sail and the helm in the refrains, gradually filling with the force of their intent.

The day came when we had decided to set out to sea. We launched our vessels and the crews went on board and everyone sat in their allotted place. The oars were placed in the rowlocks and the waters foamed with the strength of our strokes. The race between us stretched out across the calm surface of the bay, the men shouting out music and keeping time with their strokes until the pinnacles of the rocks appeared beyond one of the islands in the mouth of the harbour. Then the helmsmen stayed at the rear until we went out beyond the headland into the open sea.

We were not long travelling before the wind blew up into a gale and darkness came down from the skies. Our fleet was blown off course and our sails were torn to shreds. Day and night we battled over the tumultuous waves until the storm died down and we sailed warily under cloud and spray and rain. The wind softened and with nightfall we found ourselves ploughing through a thick fog without even light from the moon, hidden behind the clouds. The only sound was the lapping of water and the creaking of the oars in their locks. When morning came we heard a deep pounding sound coming from the north-west. 'The roar of wave on sand' we said to ourselves, and we had hardly seen the breakers before us when we had to get the boats ready to land. We jumped out and drenched to the skin as we were we fell asleep on the grey, sandy seashore.

When we woke up and cast lots to see who would do some reconnaissance, we saw a small group of men, about one hundred warriors, and we did not trust them much. But many more arrived and we were made captive. We found out that we had been captured by Fomorians. They turned us into slaves and made us do their digging and their ploughing. Our only shelter was in hovels fit for animals and they forbade us from reciting the prayers of our ancestors. They took from us our tallest and leanest youths and they were put slaving away in the forges, for the brigands were metal workers who cared only for wealth and possessions. There was confusion and terror on my companions and it was as if their bondage had sent them into a deep sleep. But this was not the fate I had in mind for this people, that they would die like slaves and be swept away out of history as if they had never existed. So I would speak to them in their hovels under the cover of night or a group would come together in a hut on a moonlit night. And I re-awakened the longing for the blessed island in their closed minds. The light went out from me until here and there someone would become inflamed with the passion and the night became littered with small groups, in mountain huts, in the shanty towns, in the shacks by the forges. And our people again were like a deathly still lake mirroring the stars of the sky.

But with the return of hope, the young became impatient and they used to rise up against the tyrant whenever they got a chance. The only end to it was defeat and brutality. And our masters devoured the bodies of our companions, and made sacrifices of them to their own gods, the gods of wealth and conquest. And I forbade my followers from continuing on with this barbarous struggle because another idea was taking shape in my resourceful mind.

I advised them to give in completely to their masters, or at least give the impression they were doing so. They should be thankful for the crumbs that were thrown their way; give praise to their great virtues and their goodness; imitate their customs; reduce themselves to nothing in the eyes of the conquerors. It was painful for me to give this advice, to my own family that was shaped in my own image, because it was a blow to my pride to pretend I was nobody, even for the sake of liberty and free passage. My regret would have been even greater if I had understood then what I understand now, that it is a great misfortune to turn humans into lapdogs as some of them never lose the habit.

Gradually my plan was working. The oppressors were made to feel that there was no longer anything to fear from us. Our submissiveness and fawning were greater than their contempt ever was. These blinkered people could not read our keen minds and they were blind to what was afoot. When they thought again of the sacrifice of the best of our men to honour the gods they worshipped, as an example to the oppressed, it never occurred to these unseeing people that we would slip through their hands. We gathered together to raise a memorial stone over the burial mound of the dead and to observe the appropriate funeral rites. When we were led down to the ships to properly commemorate the fire ship, we all raised our sails and we disappeared in the morning mist as if we had never been there. We were far out to sea when we heard their roars of anger but there was little point in them noisily casting their hot iron after us or whipping up the sea with their rocks. Our boats were swifter still heading out into the great expanse and the ocean lit up behind us where our keels cut through the waters.

We travelled for a long time seeing only remote, craggy islands or shores where there were monsters, more like giants than men, threatening us from the tops of cliffs. And after the experience of violent captivity under the Fomorians, the crews were too afraid to land and rise to their challenge. We continued sailing across the endless ocean, the swelling seas howling fiercely at us or gently teasing us on a fine day. The men were falling down with hunger, and the effort of rowing had exhausted their energies. Some of them even began to regret that we had left that place of tyranny because at least they had enough to eat back then. I was learning that there is no greater sickness of the heart than slavery and that it plants a poison that goes to the very depths of the soul.

Until at last we came within sight of land, a beautiful, peaceful country where there appeared to be no living being. The crews let out a great shout of relief and hope but we rowed cautiously along the coast for a long time before we allowed ourselves to set foot on land. All that could be seen were green forests alive with the song of a thousand birds and grass-rich pastures with deer grazing in them that looked as they never heard the sound of a hunter's horn. We hid our boats in a creek and almost immediately fell asleep. When the morning clouds reddened with a new day we set off inland looking for food and shelter. We hacked our way through the undergrowth and walked through the stately arcade of the forest. And suddenly we came out onto a stony platform and the whole country was spread out before our eyes. In the bottom half of the glen we could see the bright royal residence, the shining streams winding their way through the gardens and squares and the blue smoke rising softly from the roofs. We moved cautiously towards it but there was no guard at the gates or lookout on the ramparts. As we drew closer, the eyes of my poor sailors opened wide in amazement at the wealth and the luxury on display in the halls and it was not long before some of them began to say that they would not mind being captives forever if they could spend their lives surrounded by all this splendour. For the sturdy hope had weakened in the hearts of those who would never be happy until they had overlords to teach them lessons.

Translated from the Irish by Michael Cronin

Gianni Celati

Gianni Celati, born in 1937, is a writer, critic, film-maker and translator (from English and French). His first book, *Comiche*, appeared in 1970. He has since published several novels and collections of short stories. In 2006 the collection *Vite di pascolanti* was awarded the prestigious Viareggio Prize for fiction. This story, 'Notizie ai Naviganti', appeared in the collection *Cinema naturale* (Feltrinelli, 2001).

Marine Forecast

This is the story of a doctor who used to go sailing with a friend every Sunday, and who had an adventure in which he was possessed by voices. One night some years ago, he was on the home leg of a sailing trip with his friend and their respective wives. It was his turn to be at the helm, while the others slept in the berths below. The moon was shining, the sea was calm, and the usual breeze was blowing from the shore. In the dark, the doctor heard voices speaking clearly. Since he was alone, you can imagine how astonished he was—so much so that he just stood there, dazed, holding his breath without understanding what was happening.

They were female voices, very clear, as though they were speaking right behind him. In fact, they were coming from the land, at least ten kilometres away, carried by a wind current that made the phenomenon possible. After his initial surprise, the doctor realised that it was a conversation between two distant women. He could clearly make out the voices of an older woman and a younger one, perhaps her daughter. Probably they were talking out in the open. In the brief time that the channel was open through the wind currents that met and mingled from there to the coast, he managed to grasp or imagine a great many things. From what he heard he understood that the two women were quite poor, and that the daughter needed an operation for kidney stones. This would put them into difficulties since they didn't have any kind of welfare assistance.

It might seem strange that he managed to figure all this out, but it so happened that our doctor worked on cases like that every day, since he was a kidney specialist. There in the moonlight, he was able to picture the situation, and even formulate a diagnosis for the young woman. Once the voices disappeared, he was unable to think about anything else, not moving from the helm, even after his watch was over. He says that he felt fascinated by the young woman's voice. It was the voice of a very proud woman, one he wanted to help. How? It so happened that his hospital had just acquired a new, inexpensive medicine, which they were trialling, and which dissolved kidney stones without the need for an operation. The treatment was free, since they were studying its side-effects.

He is a man who has always wanted to help others, and this is his biggest fault, he says. Even though his turn at the helm was over, he stayed there, thinking, and the idea came to him of tracking down the young woman, even though he didn't know where or how. He wanted to search for her, explain the treatment to her, and offer a free solution to her problems. He believed the two women must be living on the stretch of coast opposite, and they must be traceable, one way or another. He says that all of a sudden his brain started working at top speed, opening itself up to ideas that would otherwise have seemed strange or embarrassing to him. In actual fact, everything in his life, including his friend and his wife and the sailing boat, was set up to prevent him from having these kinds of ideas. His was an airless world, he says, where he suffered from headaches and mild states of mental confusion. It wouldn't have been a good idea to tell the story of the voices to his friend, who was only interested in the sailboat, nor to his wife, who got jealous very easily. He didn't talk to anyone about it. The trip came to an end in the usual anticlimax of homecoming, and the next day the doctor went back to work at the hospital as usual.

A few weeks went by. One afternoon, without really thinking about it, he got into his car and drove as far as _____, looking for the place from which he had heard the night voices. On the coast, which was already deserted at that time of year, he wandered around without knowing who to ask. Half-empty cafés, blocks of homes that looked abandoned, commercial signs with no one to read them, and little shops displaying lilos and water-wings in the shape of swans, with bored salespeople and no customers. Seeing all this mundane melancholy persuaded him to change direction. Apart from anything else, the two women must have been poor, so they couldn't be living in a tourist area like this. They must live in the wilder, less populated countryside inland. And so he decided to continue his search away from the coast, starting with the old houses that appear along the dusty roads. Old, crumbling houses, lost among the fields, as far as the horizon that rises up towards the profile of the hills. On the horizon there in front of him, empty as far as the eye could see, you could just make out the occasional pond with water lilies, jonquils and swamp reeds in bloom.

He would go from farmyard to farmyard, knocking on one door after another, to ask about a certain Milena, suffering from kidney stones. Brooding over the voices he had heard that night, it had suddenly occurred to him that the young woman was called Milena. But he wasn't at all certain that was her name, he just had the feeling he had heard it in the air, that's all. Or else he had dreamed it up in one of the nocturnal visions that accompanied his house-to-house search. They were visions of farmyards, of abandoned hamlets, of dogs barking, of old women with walking sticks in dark huts like the Sibyl's cave. He was dreaming a lot at night now, something that was new for our doctor. Everything was up in the air, he had no clues except the name, and the inhabitants of the farmhouses didn't understand what he was looking for.

'Who are you looking for?'—'Someone called Milena.'—'Milena who?'—'I don't know, someone who suffers from kidney stones.'—'There's nobody like that here.'—'Have you heard of anyone round here like that?'—'But what are you looking for, why don't you tell us?' In the end they would get suspicious. They would take him for someone casing the area to burgle people's homes, or a travelling salesman who would eventually try to sell them something. The farming folk had faces that were too severe for him, a short, delicate, chubby man, with the beginnings of an ulcer to boot. He would have to get back into his car in a big hurry, anxious and embarrassed, he says. The old people looked wizened to him, and there were no young people around. The women dressed in black flapped their arms strangely to shoo away flies, or thoughts, or to show that they didn't have time to talk to him. Dogs barked in the farmyards wherever he went.

He would walk away unsteadily, his mind filled with visions of life in those places. For example the idea that there

were dark caverns inhabited by witches, like Sybils. Or else
he would see himself in the big kitchens of the farmhouses,
touching one of the black-clad women. He would be touching
her under her petticoats, he would touch her breasts and
drag her over to a bed to mount her hurriedly and then flee.
These were the visions that haunted him on certain days as
he drove through the countryside, the doctor says. There
were days when he felt possessed, and he began to tire of
this punishment, but driving randomly here and there in his
car as soon as he had a half-day off, he grew increasingly
fond of the name, Milena. He says that the more he thought
about it, the more it seemed like the right name, because it
sounded right to his ear. As soon as he said it to himself, he
could hear the proud voice of the woman he was looking
for. He seemed to hear it close by, the way it had reached
him from that unknown point on land. He had only to stop
on a road in the middle of the countryside, sitting in his car
with his head between his hands trying to concentrate, and
it was as if he could clearly hear that voice from the land,
like listening to it on the radio.

He searched the countryside for the unknown Milena right
through autumn, driving around two or three afternoons
a week, without ever talking about it to anyone. At the
beginning of winter he stopped, because his search was
really just too foolish, he says. He had also caught bronchitis,
along with a touch of lumbago, which made him limp a bit.
But when spring returned, so did his reverie, along with
his hay fever, and once again he felt possessed, constantly
daydreaming about the voice he had heard on the boat. 'I'm
possessed, I'm possessed,' he would say to himself, as he
took the wrong turn at every crossroad, sneezing non-stop.
And now he was calling in sick to the hospital so he could
hunt for the unknown Milena, starting from the tourist
areas on the coast once again.

It was the middle of spring, but driving along the coastline our doctor saw everything around him as grey, among processions of holiday houses, holiday hotels, holiday shops, marine outfitters and meeting places populated only during the summer. It seemed like an uninhabited planet, with pointless advertising signs that stare at you everywhere you turn, useless street lights that come on at sunset. Avenues squared off by angular facades and miserable trees suffocating in the middle of a desert of asphalt. He would listen to conversations in the cafés and hear people talking about lottery wins, about new brands of cars, about football games, about rich and famous people. A world without air, he says. But now his own life also seemed hopeless to him, like that of someone surprised by a storm far from any shelter. It was hopeless living with his wife, to whom he had nothing to say, and with his unpleasant children who were doing badly at school, and with his friend who talked only about sailing, and with his conceited head physician, who wanted to buy a hill-top village. Yes, a whole village just for him, carried away by the delirium of new wealth that was circulating among all the doctors of his department.

The doctor went around narrating his life to himself, as everyone does, no doubt, telling themselves their lives to show that they're right. But to prove absolutely that he was right, he really had to find the unknown Milena, or some other woman with that proud voice he thought he could still hear. This was the voice of the woman who was supposed to change his life, according to the palm reader, Egle. Because this was what was going to happen one day, he would change his life and take off on his own road, as if it had all already been decreed. The palm reader Egle was certainly of that opinion, and he went to consult her once a week, on Wednesday afternoons, in a dusty room full of dried flowers, accessed through the ruins of a villa surrounded by weeds, in the old quarter of his city.

The headaches that tormented him and the beginnings of an ulcer he just couldn't cure also dissuaded him from continuing to wander around haphazardly in search of an unknown woman. Now he began to search for her methodically. Egle steered him towards points she located on her map with her magic pendulum. And by the beginning of spring he had already marked out an area of the countryside to look for traces of the unknown Milena. But wherever he was, the doctor would stop and listen, hoping to hear voices like the ones he had heard on the sailboat in the night. He needed to hear voices from the land. Another clairvoyant, or rather fortune-teller, by the name of Marilù, had confirmed for him that those voices were his destiny.

He was a short, chubby man, with a frightened look about him, and certainly possessed by something. By this stage he was impatient with his colleagues at the hospital and with his family at home. Because of the change that destiny seemed to have promised him, he was often rude and abrupt. On some evenings, coming out of the hospital, he would go for a drive along the coast, just to put his head out the car window and yell to the wind: 'I want voices from the land, voices from the land! My God, please, I'm begging you!' And afterwards he would feel very foolish, that is, so completely foolish that it seemed to him useless to stay on this earth.

He didn't know what he was looking for, nor did he question himself about it, and he didn't talk about it to anyone, apart from the palm reader Egle, whom he visited every Wednesday afternoon. The map searches with the pendulum were the only way to discover where the mysterious Milena might be living. According to the fortune-teller

Marilù, she must be sick and in need of help. The cards
told her that. The mysterious Milena would often appear
as the High Priestess, according to Signora Marilù. 'See
here?'—'What?'—'The High Priestess, do you see what
she has next to her?'—'No, what?'—'This is the card of
misfortunes.'—'For whom?'—'The woman you're looking
for, do you see the two of spades?'—'Yes.'—'And this one
is you, you will help her out of them.'

I try to imagine these dialogues with the fortune-teller,
a middle-aged peroxide blonde, fat and effusive, with a lot
of lipstick, who always gave him favourable predictions.
They were so favourable that he thought of almost nothing
else, he says, forgetting everything and paying no attention
to the contours of things. He forgot meeting places and
times of day, finding himself to his surprise at the hospital
attending to his patients, or on his own driving through
the empty countryside, or else with his family at the dinner
table, eating soup in silence. He would find himself here
or there, doing everything mechanically, immersed in
his thoughts and presentiments. But he says that nobody
noticed, since he was more efficient and precise than ever
at work, and he also seemed more serious and responsible
at home, thanks to his sleepwalking state.

We come now to an important moment in the story. It is
autumn again. In the empty countryside, a few kilometres
from the shore, there is an area towards which the palm
reader Egle had been directing the doctor for some time
by way of the pendulum revolving over the map. Along a
country road just before you get to the foothills, there is an
open space covered with broken asphalt and bordered by a
barbed wire fence. Beyond the fence and on the other side
of the open space are the cement ruins of a long-abandoned
factory. Rusty iron supports stick up like warts among
fragments of concrete. An old, nameless ruin, exposed to

the winds and the rain. There are tall weeds growing in the holes in the asphalt and on top of the cement blocks. But why did the doctor get the idea that the voices he had heard on the sailboat must have come from these ruins? Not exactly from the ruins, he says, but from behind the ruins.

In a café-tobacconist in the nearest village, the one-eyed proprietor, on hearing that he was looking for someone called Milena, asked: 'Milena who? Milena the giantess?'—'I don't know, it must be someone who suffers from kidney problems.'—'Well, Milena is sick, but I don't know what from.'—'And where does she live?'—'Where the old factory was, but behind it, on the canal.' This is what our doctor says, and here I imagine him in an unfashionable raincoat, his shoulders bowed, looking tired. At that time he had also developed a touch of asthma, and frequently had trouble breathing. In any case, the place the tobacconist suggested fitted with the area the palm reader Egle had identified by means of the pendulum, and with the ideas the doctor had formed in the night on the sailing boat. In other words, it was within about twenty kilometres of the place from which the voices might have reached him from the land. For a whole afternoon he tried to find a way to the back of the ruins, following the tobacconist's instructions, but without managing to locate the maintenance track he needed to take, in the labyrinth of dusty roads.

On that autumn evening, he once again found himself near the barbed wire, in front of the factory ruins. As night fell, he heard the voices from the land. Or else he believed he heard them, because he would often will himself into that hallucination. The air was completely still, neither warm nor cold. It was about to rain and a few drops were already falling. He bent and put his ear to the ground, on the asphalt. Sweat began to dampen his forehead, he says, at the thought that the famous Milena was a stone's throw

away and that he was finally going to meet her. Taking a
torch, he slipped under the barbed wire, past the clumps of
weeds, and past the ruins of the abandoned factory. Behind
these ruins appeared one of those little country houses with
an external chimney of crumbling bricks. It was an old, low
house, sunk in the shadows beside the canal, at the end of
the maintenance track he had been searching for.

What happened next that evening, I don't know. It seems
to me that the doctor had a memory lapse, or perhaps he
just never wanted to talk about it. It doesn't matter, let's
carry on. A few months went by, and in the spring our
doctor started writing the story of what had happened to
him over the previous year. He told how one night on the
sailboat he had heard voices from the land, and wrote about
his efforts to trace the mysterious Milena, and the thoughts
that had come to him as he searched for her through the
countryside. Whenever he was on night duty at the hospital,
he would closet himself in his office and spend the night
writing, quite happily, he says. He also wanted to unburden
himself by talking about what he couldn't tell anyone, stuck
in a life that seemed hopeless, with his wife unhappy about
his absences and his children more and more stupefied in
front of the television, and his conceited head physician
increasingly lost in the delirium of new wealth.

Every evening after work, he travelled many kilometres
to reach the little house on the bank of the canal, with its
external chimney and its crumbling walls. Coming from
the maintenance track, he would see the mother of the
said Milena eyeing him from the window. She was one
of those black-clad countrywomen, and as soon as he got
out of the car, he would find her standing on the doorstep,
staring at him and greeting him with a nod. He says that
he felt embarrassed by her scrutiny and would hurry his
pace. The woman would remain in the shadow holding his

gaze, as though he were an unpredictable animal you have to keep an eye on. She was heavy, broad, dressed in black with a black petticoat down to her knees, and black socks that reached to just below the knee. It wasn't clear whether she was in mourning or whether she had been dressed in mourning all her life, says the doctor.

When he sat down to drink coffee at the kitchen table, he would see her moving about, her hips swinging heavily, without ever speaking to him and always turning her eyes away if she realised he was looking at her. Then she would pass him pieces of paper where she had written down all the things she had bought, the amounts for meat, bread, illustrated newspapers, medicines and biscuits for her daughter, with the daily total to pay. The doctor would put the money on the table as he finished his coffee, then go to see the daughter. She was a giantess over two metres tall. She rarely emerged from the bedroom because she was very ill, very weak, fat and indolent. The doctor rarely saw her standing up, and when he examined her she would look at him with her eyelids half closed, before tiredly turning her eyes away. It seemed as though the two women always considered him an intruder, he says, despite his efforts to help them, to treat the daughter, and to provide for their needs. In fact he has always wanted to help others, and this is his biggest fault, he says, or rather his misfortune.

The doctor was treating the daughter for the after-effects of an operation on her gall bladder. He checked up on her every day, asking her questions to which she would only mutter in reply, tiredly, as if he were disturbing her for no reason, and she didn't want him even to touch her wrist to check her pulse. If he so much as reached out a hand, she reacted wildly, shying violently away from his touch. The doctor would have to turn to the mother to get some indication of the daughter's symptoms, and then he would listen to the two women's exchange in dialect, without understanding a single word. He would get tired of asking, he says, and give up on the questions, tired of always wanting to help others.

After the operation on her gall bladder, the giantess could hardly eat anything anymore. She got by on biscuits crumbled into tea or into sweetened hot water, and she stayed in bed all day dressed in an old blue tracksuit, flicking through illustrated newspapers or watching television. The doctor never heard her complete two sentences, except when she spoke in dialect with her mother. He says she seemed indifferent to everything, sunk in the indolence of a fat, slow-witted girl. She can't have been even thirty years old, but as she was so gigantic, it was hard to tell her age, apart from her face, which was already faded. While the doctor was examining her, she would lie on her side, keeping her eyes on the television screen, hurriedly muttering answers or sighing as though he were a great bore. At length he would leave, dejected, without so much as a goodbye from her.

Around the house at night you could hear bird calls, the rustling of bushes, sometimes the lapping of the canal, and often before getting back into the car, the doctor felt the urge to take a walk in the dark as far as the ruined factory, as far as the asphalt and the barbed wire. When he got back he would spy from the shadows on the two women in their room. He was spellbound by something, he says, always possessed and under the influence of others. In the room the daughter would be stretched out on the bed in front of the television, immobile, inert, tall and broad, with her long tangled hair, a giantess with a face that was beginning to wilt, although it was still young and rosy. The mother, by contrast, would be kneeling on the bed doing strange exercises with her arms reaching up over her head, as though she were invoking help from the heavens, and only after a long time did the doctor realise that it must be some kind of gymnastics.

Here I see the doctor as very hesitant, wearing a shapeless raincoat, his baldness very pronounced by this stage, getting back into the car and asking himself the same questions each evening. He would wonder if the Milena he had found was really the woman he had sought for so long. Well, she was called Milena, but she didn't suffer from kidney stones, it was gall stones. And was her voice the same as the one he had heard in the night? Perhaps, but this woman muttered and spoke very little, so it was hard to make the comparison. What is more, the fortune-teller Marilù had changed her interpretation of events, and according to her the cards said that this wasn't the woman of his destiny. The doctor couldn't grasp his destiny, and kept asking for explanations. 'Look here, do you see this card?'—'Yes, what does it mean?'—'Beware of women who make you think one thing is another.'—'Like who?'—'Like Egle, who sent you to those two.'—'But why? Is she conning me?'—'She's like a succubus, she does everything to keep you tied to her, and to worm cash out of you, along with those two women.'

Without believing Signora Marilù, whom he visited on Friday evenings, was wrong, he really wanted to continue his consultations with the palm reader Egle, because by this point she was the only person who thought he was right. She assured him that this Milena was definitely the person he had been looking for, since the pendulum now always returned unhesitatingly to that same point. Then, every evening, late at night, when he got home, the fights with his wife would begin again. His children looked at him as if he were some kind of weirdo, perhaps a drunk. But why could he not cut himself loose? Because he was possessed, he says, under the influence of others, from which you can never escape. And also because he is someone who has always wanted to help others, even when it wasn't in his interests, he says. Because he was possessed, one fine day he decided that life could just do what it wanted, he didn't care. From then on, he would just do whatever happened along, from day to day, under the influence of others, or swept along by events. If other people think they are in charge of life, good luck to them, he didn't believe in it any more. He would let himself go, do everything his destiny wanted, even if he didn't understand what this whole story of having a destiny meant.

Apart from anything else, by now the doctor could no longer hear the voices from the land that had been echoing in his mind when he went in search of the unknown Milena. Often the phone would ring at the hospital and discouraging voices would sound in his ear, abstract, starchy voices, as though every sentence were a pose. Then the desire to hear the voices from the land would come back to him: voices from the land! He would pray to God to send him some voices from the land once again, rather than always just voices from above, voices from the television, voices of the eternal fathers, or apathetic voices quoting only hard facts so as to avoid being contradicted, or else voices of people who want to be someone and so imitate the voice of someone else.

The giantess was always in bed, delicate and obese, and also sulky as soon as he would enter the room. Precisely because he felt rejected, the doctor says, he felt an increasing desire to be part of her life, perhaps even to marry her or become her servant. He brought her gifts: boxes of chocolates, or clothes so that she would get changed rather than just lie in bed all the time in her tracksuit. He would come into the room with the gift, show it to her without speaking, and she would point a finger to tell him to leave it there on the chair, and go right back to watching the television on the chest of drawers. The room smelled of stale air, sweat, dirty sheets and dead flowers, but it didn't bother him. On the contrary, he says that the stench gave him the only sensation of intimacy with the giantess that he managed to achieve. The black-clad mother was always surveying the scene, as though afraid he would assault her daughter. The doctor would have to ask her: 'How is Milena?' The mother would barely answer: 'Today she was nauseous; she can't bring herself to eat anything.' The chocolates were clearly out of place, inappropriate for the sick woman. The mother would eat them. By now the doctor was just pretending to be treating the giantess, as doctors at the hospital often do, he says.

It is also strange that, from the very first day, neither of the women asked him why he was interested in them. They hadn't asked him why he had offered to take the giantess to hospital for her gall bladder operation, and why he came to see her every day, why he paid their bills, or why he had paid for their roof to be fixed. It was as if all of this were normal. They had never asked who he was, what he wanted from them, nor had they thanked him even once. The mother watched him every moment, without turning her head, out of the corner of her eye. Two or three times, the doctor talked with the mother in the kitchen after he had visited the sick woman, trying to figure out if they were the women he had heard from the sailboat. The conversations were unsustainable, since the mother barely answered, sighing with exhaustion. At times she would let him talk on, getting up and moving her heavy hips, her wide haunches, as if to show all the flesh she was carrying around under her clothes. That was the impression she gave him, and he says he got excited watching her. Then she would come back and sit down, looking in the other direction, as though she was annoyed by his insistence. She didn't understand what he wanted to know. 'What voices?'—'Some voices that I heard one night.'—'Where?'—'Offshore, I was on a boat.'—'So?'—'I wanted to know if they were your voices.'—'When?'—'Two years ago.'—'I don't know.'

The following day he would go back to the palm reader Egle, for fresh reinforcement. But at a certain point it seemed to him that even Egle was tired of him, tired of having to keep repeating the same things to him. He also realised that she didn't look anything like a Sibyl, since she was dressed more or less like a dancing girl, with bracelets and veils, perfumes and aromas that wrapped themselves around her in the ruined room, under the leaky roof. The fortune-teller Marilù made less of a performance of it, but she didn't change her interpretation of events. She would repeat that this was not the Milena he was looking for. One day the doctor asked her: 'But where is my destiny?'—'What destiny?'—'The one that was in the cards.'—'Forget about the cards, believe me: they're conning you.' Now she no longer talked to him as a sorceress, but as someone who wants to show her professional honesty and not deceive a client. She no longer remembered that she had promised him a destiny, and so he stopped going to see her on Friday evenings. Apart from everything else, she didn't look at all like a Sibyl, or at least not like the Sibyls he had seen in his nocturnal visions, back when he was scouring the countryside.

He had heard that in the mountains there really was an old Sibyl, who lived in a dark cavern, cured people and read their destinies in melted lead in a basin. She was up in the mountains that you could see in the distance from the house of the two women, beyond the hills. One day he left the hospital late in the morning, because he wanted to go to look for the old Sibyl and get the truth. Around one o'clock he arrived at the ruins of the concrete factory, which looked increasingly crumbling. The parts made of concrete looked as though they were rotting under the sun. He decided to stop here and ask for directions from the giantess's mother, so as to not get lost in the unfamiliar mountains. When he arrived at the house, he realised that the mother must not be there, as he couldn't see her bicycle. The door was slightly open; everything else was normal, with not a sound to be heard.

He went into the kitchen; everything was silent. He saw the bedroom door slightly open. Peering in from the doorway, he saw the giantess asleep on the bed. He had never seen her asleep, nor had he ever seen her wearing any other clothes than her tracksuit. Now she was wearing a floral dress he had given her; that is, he had given her the material and her mother had sewn it for her. She was curled up on her side, with her knees almost up to her face, and her large thighs exposed in that position. The cleft between her buttocks was also exposed, between two masses of flaccid, translucent flesh. She was holding her thumb close to her mouth, as though she had just been sucking it. Often, examining her, the doctor had seen her with her thumb in her mouth, putting it between her partly closed lips without sucking it. Now, curled up on her side, she was holding her thumb close to her lips. But she was so relaxed and peaceful in her enormous body, her breath so light in her sleep, that he couldn't stop peering at her. He went into the room, into that smell of dead flowers, sheets, dirty clothes and sweat. On the bed around her were scattered pins, dolls, necklaces, bracelets, rings. The monumental sleeping girl had some little rings lying close to her lap, as though she had been playing at putting them on until just before.

He sat there on a chair, gazing at her. She didn't move. Everything around them, the whole world around the house and reaching to the sky was calm and stilled at that moment. He says that at that moment everything was in order, despite the mess in the room, with socks on the floor, a dirty teaspoon, the remains of crumbled biscuits on the bed, magazines abandoned on the chair. You just needed to be still and everything became calm and free from desire, without you having to ask yourself any more if life was going well or badly. He says that he had an urge to go to sleep, he had forgotten about the Sibyl in the mountains. Actually, it seems he had the feeling he had already been to the cave of the Sibyl who was supposed to tell him his destiny. There are things you can't explain, he says, and here I'll present them as they come to mind. The doctor had a great urge to go to sleep, looking at the giant girl who lay so deeply asleep on the bed, with a face that he now recognised; she, too, was free from desire. A face like a celluloid doll's: oval, with a small mouth like a doll's. The face of a little girl who has never grown up, but full of wrinkles, as though under the rosy surface her skin was that of an old woman's.

But just as he thought that perhaps she might be the Sibyl, he realised that the mother was glaring at him from the doorway. He started, and immediately left the room, embarrassed. He didn't know what to do. The mother kept looking at him as though he'd been up to some sort of prank. He says that her stare insinuated that he had wanted to rape the giantess, or touch her or something like that. In any case, it was certainly a reproof for having been found in her daughter's room. The mother closed the bedroom door, slowly, then put two plates on the table, watching him all the time. He didn't know whether to go or stay; he was extremely embarrassed by her staring. Then the woman invited him to have some soup, ladling it into a bowl and pointing to it with a hurried gesture. The doctor wasn't hungry, but he ate all the same. Then the mother told him he had to split some wood, like an order that is not to be questioned. And for the whole afternoon, he split wood in the open space behind the house. By evening he had a sore back and aching bones, as well as a headache. He had worked so hard with the hatchet that he wobbled as he walked, and asked if he could lie down.

The mother pointed him to the old sofa with the springs coming out of the fabric, where he fell into a deep sleep. When he woke it was evening, and on the table there was a plate of cold soup, evidently left there for him. The two women were in the bedroom, from where he could hear the sound of the television. The doctor ate. He still felt very tired, with a headache, and no desire to go home. He got a blanket from his car and slept on the uncomfortable sofa.

The next day was Sunday, he didn't need to go to the hospital, and as soon as he woke up the mother began giving him non-stop orders, without looking him in the face, but watching him out of the corner of her eye, with gestures and words that intimidated him. First she made him light the fire, then she sent him to the village to do the shopping, then up onto the roof with the ladder to put some tiles back in place, then to take away an old bird's nest from the chimney opening. In the afternoon she showed him a mountain of linens to take to the storeroom, where there was a wash tub full of steaming water. After stirring the clothes in the wash tub, he went to hang them out on the lines in front of the house.

He says that he was starting to feel liverish, with a bit of nausea, as well as his headache and a toothache. In the evening he had no appetite, but ate the usual soup. All he wanted was to run away, but he was completely worn out. In the days that followed, the mother continuously gave him orders, the way people talk to servants. She didn't even give him time to check on her daughter, and put him straight to work again as soon as he entered the house. But why did he go back to that house? I don't know. As it was, he had to carry the firewood into the house, shift and wash the demijohn bottles, destroy the mole tunnels, spread insecticide for the cockroaches in the storeroom, hoe the vegetable garden, cut the weeds, wash the bottles for the tomato preserves, peel the potatoes, clean the fireplace and do lots of other jobs that I can't remember. As soon as he finished one job, the woman would give him another order with a couple of sharp words, and he would obey without knowing why. Every time he just stood there in surprise, then he watched her leave, moving her big behind in the black dress, waddling ponderously away. But it always happened that she would turn around and catch him in his clumsy staring. It seemed as though she could read his mind. She dominated him even when she was looking the other way. More uncomfortable than ever, with his headache and his toothache, the doctor remembered that the fortune-teller Marilù had foretold that he would become the victim of two succubi.

But then even going back to his own house he felt at the mercy of the succubus mother dressed in black, as though he were still receiving her orders even there. He felt he had to do everything in a hurry at the hospital so he could race back to receive more orders in the house by the canal. Meanwhile, he felt his arms becoming flabby, his baldness was rapidly gaining ground on the top of his skull, and he didn't have time to go to the dentist to have his teeth seen to. He no longer exchanged so much as a word with his colleagues at the hospital, except when absolutely necessary, and they looked on him as a failure, a poor fool who would never get on in his career. When he went home, his wife would be in a huff with him for hours, then suddenly she would burst out into sighs of: 'But where do you go? Where do you spend the night? Do you have a lover? Tell me, so at least I can resign myself to it.' The only thing that occurred to him to reply was: 'Why don't I die? Why don't I die?'

He did not want to stay at home any more, and he announced to his wife that he had a lover and was going to stay with her. But he said it to her over the telephone so he wouldn't find himself at the mercy of her crying, since others had the power to dominate him completely. In the house on the canal he disliked sleeping on the uncomfortable sofa with the springs which poked his back. He said so to the giantess's mother and one evening she took the kerosene lamp and took him into the ruins of the factory, where on the first floor there was a big concrete room full of rubble, with a camp bed in a corner. Someone must have slept or lived there, because you could see the ashes of a campfire, some charred wood, and the windows covered up with sheets of plastic. While they were in the room, with the kerosene lamp resting on the pavement spreading a weak light amid the shadows, the doctor says he realised that he was a slave. Not only the victim of a succubus, but a slave to the situation he had created through his mania for helping others. Nor could he go home, because there he would be the slave of the other situation that he had created with his family.

The black-clad mother put a blanket on the camp bed, and he watched her from behind, in a state of confusion. Her large buttocks, with the flesh trembling under her dress, would get him excited at certain moments. When she passed close to him, he stretched out a hand to touch her, brushing her side. She didn't say anything, but turned to glare at him, waiting for his next move. Then the doctor says that the idea flashed into his mind of overturning the situation, of buying her and keeping her on a leash, using her greed as leverage. He pulled out some large denomination banknotes from his wallet and put them on the camp bed. He was shaking all over, he says, but he wanted to get the better of her, bend her to his will, and finally understand what his destiny was. Embarrassed as he was by the situation, not even he knows how he was able to pluck up the courage to nod towards the bed. She understood, took the money and tucked it between her breasts, then started taking off her dress, always keeping an eye on him, then finally let him mount her in silence on the camp bed. She did all this without so much as a sigh or a pant, making him even more of a slave with her muteness, then dressing herself again calmly and going off without saying anything.

The same thing happened again twice, then he didn't feel like it any more. When, certain evenings, she would look at him expectantly, he would simply give her the money. Then she stopped even looking at him that way, since he would just give her all the money he earned at the hospital, minus what he had to give his wife for so-called alimony. In the house on the canal he and the mother had become like husband and wife, he says, apart from the fact that they didn't sleep together and never talked to one another. He always slept on the camp bed in the ruined factory, and obeyed all the orders he received from the black-clad mother. Now it seemed as though the giantess treated him like a father or an uncle, and even though she never spoke to him, she no longer huffed and puffed when she found him beside her. However, he was afraid of stopping to look at her, as he would have liked to, because the mother would have turned her hard eyes on him right away, mortifying him completely. In any case he had already understood his destiny; he no longer needed to consult the Sybil.

That area of the countryside offers no consolation and nothing to hope for. From his bunker you would be able to see the stars, and perhaps also the lights of the houses up on the mountain, if the windows weren't covered up with plastic sheets. In the big cement room full of rubble, with scattered ashes and a fire lit on the floor, in the silence of the night you can hear the cries of a nocturnal bird. We now come to the winter evening when his friend went to get him, and found him with a fever. Seated beside the fire, the two men project shadows that tremble along with the flames because of the draughts coming up from below. In the dim light, the doctor, dressed in worn-out clothes, seems like a gaunt old tramp. His friend knows that by this stage they are keeping him on at the hospital only out of the goodness of the vain chief physician's heart. The doctor has finished writing the story of all this and he wants his friend to read it here, beside the fire. So the other man begins reading, seated on a fruit crate, while outside the snow falls, and the doctor shakes from his fever, with his right leg aching from rheumatism. Not long ago the giantess sent her mother to ask for him, because she didn't feel well. But the doctor wants to stay in the big room beside the fire until his friend finishes reading his story, and so he chased the black-clad woman off with a couple of hysterical shrieks.

It is cold, and the fire doesn't warm him. While his friend reads the story, the doctor remembers the people on the pier—workers, strikers, wanderers, he doesn't know who they were—who had stood there against the morning sky, against the clouds, against the white horses of the sea that rose up in great tall waves. The friend doesn't know what he's talking about. Perhaps he's talking about something he saw on television, when he went to the two women's house in the evenings to warm himself a little. The doctor says that those people must still be there on the pier, waiting. 'What are they waiting for?' He doesn't answer. He says there's no longer any place for people like him in the world, for what he believed he was, for what he used to think. He adds: 'We believed we were above everything, but we are like everyone else, like the animals, like the birds, like the cows at the manger.' And his friend notices that these words also seem as though they have emerged from a television set. They are not voices from the land.

Now there is only the cold of winter, which our doctor feels even more because he eats little and is constantly sneezing, shut up here in the big concrete room. His camp bed is a mass of dirty, rumpled sheets and he is wearing the only blanket he has. The mother brings him something to eat every day, but not much, just a plate of soup and a bit of bread and butter. And the less he eats, the colder he feels, naturally, while there against the breakwater the waves rise, and the sea rages along the whole coast, according to the news on the radio for the past few days. Part of the coast has been flooded, but by this stage the whole coast is at the mercy of the sea, says the doctor. Thirty or forty kilometres are nothing but desert with no shelter.

His friend has finished reading the story. The doctor says that he doesn't want to hear his comments; he hates comments. But he would like his story to be published, because then someone might read it and write to him to put him on the right track, in case the famous Milena is actually a real person and not some obsession of his. He still hopes to find out if the woman with the proud voice that had fascinated him is the indolent giantess, or somebody else, or an illusion. But to understand all this you need a lot of time, says the doctor, enough time to let yourself go and lose yourself entirely, and enough time to get back on track and look for something else. Yes, and you have to know how to keep battling on without any goal, without any desire that carries you on to ever new illusions. This is the meaning of destiny, in his opinion. At this point he adds: 'I'm so weak that I can't decide anything anymore.'

In the morning, his friend takes him back home in the car, wrapped in a blanket, pale as a corpse, his whole body shaking with fever. It's raining huge droplets, and the view is entirely grey. In that part of the countryside when it rains a lot the land beside the canals floods immediately, and then you see people fishing under their umbrellas on the many canals that intersect among the fields. You see bicycles and the occasional car disappearing in the mist, and farmhouses that appear from out of a grey haze. All that darkness and the grey of the haze over the canals seems like a spell, allowing people to live protected from the clamour of the world. But it can also produce melancholic deliriums, or other deliriums that there's no point in defining here. Perhaps it was that atmosphere that affected our doctor, trapping him in the abandoned cement factory, among the weeds that have invaded the land all around, behind the little house on the canal where the two women live. When he left home it was the end of spring, and now it is winter. It snowed during the night, and in his bunker it was freezing even next to the fire.

The doctor wakes up when they get to the coast. He trembles, then straightens up on the seat. 'Look, look!' He points to some men there on the pier next to the breakwater, while the whitecaps rise above them, tall and pale. The friend sees them too. In the distance they seem like evacuees, perhaps unemployed, perhaps just wanderers with nothing to do. The whole backdrop of the sea is leaden, apart from the white, foaming waves against the breakwater. The long pier

looks like a ribbon pushing out into the sea, in the middle
of the furious waves, and there, drawn up in a line, those
men. From a distance they look shabby, with umbrellas,
tarpaulins and newspapers over their heads, or buttoned
up in their raincoats, with their hands in their pockets,
but calm, immobile, indistinct. It's not clear what they
are doing there, huddled together in the storm. It seems as
though they are waiting for the end of everything, patiently,
without moving, surrounded by salt spray, exposed to the
tempest that rages on.

The doctor coughs, he must have pneumonia, on top of
all his other pains and ailments. His friend will have to take
him to the hospital, and at the hospital he will be at the
mercy of his colleagues in their delirium of new wealth. This
is the only solution, and it's not the best one, says the friend,
because the doctor will hate being with those people. But
I don't know what the best thing is, perhaps it's a mistake
like all the other mistakes, like all the other illusions we
chase after. The radio, which the friend has now turned on,
warns of powerful storms along the coast. You can hear
the wind howling, shaking the lamp posts, anticipating the
hurricane that's coming from the sea or from who knows
where, it doesn't much matter. All around is like a desert,
but a grey asphalt desert, between processions of holiday
houses, holiday hotels, holiday shops, marine outfitters and
meeting places populated only during the summer. You get
the impression of an uninhabited planet, its advertising
signs shaken by the wind as they watch us pass. Over the
radio a voice, which seems like the last voice on earth, is
transmitting the marine forecast.

Translated from the Italian by Sarah Hill

Park Wan-suh

Park Wan-suh (also Romanised as Pak Wan-sô and Bak Wan-seo) is by common consent the most notable female author in South Korea. Her works have not only received prestigious literary awards but have topped bestseller lists and been successfully adapted for the screen.

Park was born near Gaeseong, in what is now North Korea, in 1931. In 1970 she embarked on her career with *The Naked Tree*, a coming-of-age novel, which won a literary prize. She has since maintained an astonishingly prolific output with over 150 short stories and novellas and some twenty novels to her credit. Her debut novel *The Naked Tree* and two short story collections, *My Very Last Possession and Other Stories* and *A Sketch of the Fading Sun*, are available in English.

This text is from her novel *Geu manteon singaneun nuga da meogeosseulkka* (Who Ate Up All the Singa?).

Seoul, so far away

Grandfather's second stroke ushered in a decline in the family's fortunes. Even as a child I recognised the thickening clouds. My younger uncle and his wife had left for Seoul. They were inspired by my mother, who was a force to reckon with. She had pioneered a life in the capital, and my grandparents' resentment toward her began to soften. Actually, let me put that more accurately: their resentment began to soften once they found themselves benefiting from her ambition.

In the previous school holidays, Mother and Brother had returned home. Brother was dressed neatly in his uniform,

and Mother was the picture of confidence itself. She told
everyone that Brother had been admitted to a public school,
no mean feat. Not only that, she said, its graduates came
up with civil service jobs easily, even at the Office of the
Governor General.

I came from a rustic scholar family that was just this
side of illiterate. I'm ashamed to admit it, but Grandfather
had neither historical consciousness nor Korean pride
despite his constant boasts about our yangban status. His
aristocratic noblesse consisted in looking down on families
that occupied lower rungs in the pecking order, and his
sense of class responsibility went no further than dictating
that his sons' wives come from clans of equal status in the
so-called 'Orthodox Faction.' Whenever he sized anyone
up, he'd trot out his favourite saying: 'You can deck yourself
out however you want, but the bones give you away.'

His meagre loyalty to yangban ideals meant that even
a civil service job with Japan's colonial administration
represented high status to him, and he could dream that
his grandson, the heir who would carry on our surname,
was destined to bring glory to the clan. And if that's how
Grandfather thought, who in the family would dare scorn
my mother, whose son showed such promise of rising in
the world? All the more so, since Younger Uncle, trusting
in her support, had gone off to Seoul as well.

At that point, neither of my uncles had children; after
Younger Uncle departed, the household became drearier.
Our house was large and built with attention to detail. I'm
told that Father had constructed it before I was born, in the
belief that all three brothers, together with their parents
and their many offspring, would live under the same roof
in eternal harmony and prosperity. With fewer people
around, I had even more room for wallowing in self-pity,
and nowhere suited me and my wallowing better than the

pillar that divided the veranda in half. I'd lean against it, preoccupied, and gaze out beyond the entrance to the village. When my family caught me at this, they immediately sensed why I was so sad and lonely, especially my grandmother. She'd scramble to snuggle me and then coo huskily over and over, 'My poor baby.'

They thought I was waiting for my mother as I sat like that, and because they did, I believed it too. But it was a strange type of waiting, one I hadn't experienced before, completely devoid of the sweet restlessness that tinged my anticipation for Grandfather. 'Cheok cheok, thumb stop, middle finger, if Mother's at Wardrobe Rock Hill.' I couldn't accept that even if I played my game a hundred times my waiting might be in vain. Any time someone remarked that I looked so sad because I was pining for my mother, I'd burst into hysterical tears. The more I tried to deny it, the truer it became.

But a force stronger than my finger fortune-telling game was at work. One day Mother appeared out of the blue, even though it wasn't the holidays. I was relieved. Here was proof that she had longed for me so much she couldn't bear it! But she said that she'd come not because she missed me but to take me back with her.

'You have to go to school in Seoul too.' I couldn't decide if I liked what Mother said. I thought I might have vaguely yearned for Seoul, but I'd never imagined attending school there. My grandmother practically fainted when she heard what Mother had in mind. 'What? Sending a girl to Seoul for school?' Another dispute broke out in the family. 'What did you do to make so much money you can talk about sending her to Seoul? Did I get that right? What if somebody hears you?'

Mother stayed silent, so she continued, 'Father's only pleasure since his stroke has been watching this cute little thing come and go. And you want to take her away? How heartless can you get!'

Grandmother's shift from insult to pleading had no effect, so she switched tactics again. Confronting me, she asked, 'Who do you like better, Grandma or Mummy? Tell me right away. If it's Grandma, tell Mummy you want to live with me. Right now.'

I had only one way out. I exploded in tears. 'I don't know, I don't know,' I wailed. I couldn't cope with being torn so senselessly. Even as an adult, I hated to see children asked, 'Who do you love more, Mummy or Daddy?'

Mother put an abrupt end to this pointless dispute. She didn't have time to dawdle. Without consulting anyone, me included, she took my hair, as if she were going to comb it, and then chopped it off.

Up to that point, I'd worn my hair in tiny braids, just like the other girls in the village. Until it grew long and thick enough to be gathered into a single braid, we divided it from the top in squares, like a Chinese chessboard, and tied each patch off with brightly coloured thread or thin ribbons. The whole process took ages and needed to be repeated daily, otherwise you were left with a tangled mess. A single glance at a girl's hair told you how well valued she was at home.

My father's sister had tended to my hair until she got married, as if grooming it were her hobby. Afterward, my uncle's wife took over. She combed and plaited it so that it was neat and shiny, and I took secret pride in it. From a young age I assumed that if people commented I was pretty or cute, it was because my hair impressed them. Of all my attributes, my hair gave me the most confidence.

But Mother not only chopped off this precious, precious hair of mine, she shaved the back of my head to create a high hairline. Before I could protest, she bullied me into submission with the remark that this was how all the kids in Seoul cut their hair.

'Oh my goodness! What an awful sight!' Grandmother's jaw dropped. The feeling of so much hair missing on the back of my head was even worse than having my bangs cut in a straight line. I ventured out of the house tentatively and within seconds became the butt of my friends' ridicule.

'Nyah-nyah nyah-nyah-nyah, someone's got a face on the back of her head!'

In those days bobbed hair was cut so short it really did look as though the back of the head could have a face. But their teasing didn't bother me too much because I now had a snappy comeback. 'This is how kids in Seoul get their hair cut. But you don't know that, do you?' I was already looking down on my benighted peers. My bobbed hair not only made Grandmother surrender, it alienated me from the countryside. I wanted to leave with my mother as soon as possible.

I went to the outer quarters to say goodbye to Grandfather. He refused to look at me straight, but he seemed to know about everything that had gone on. He expressed his displeasure loudly. 'Damn awful sight is right.'

Then he rummaged through his pouch and tossed out a fifty-jeon silver coin. I felt hurt. Why did he have to throw it toward me if it was a present? I slapped the rolling coin to a stop with my palm, then grasped it and thanked him. Grandfather seemed to need consoling for his heartbreak more than I did for being insulted. I thought I'd start bawling if he showed any cracks in his gruff exterior. He snapped at me to leave right away.

What Mother did may have deserved my grandparents' anger, but she was still the senior daughter-in-law. More to the point, they had few descendants, and she was mother to the grandson who'd carry on the family line. Besides, she was a plucky woman who had the wherewithal to set up house in Seoul, where they said your nose would get stolen right off your face if you dozed off. The packages waiting outside made it clear that, whether my grandparents approved of her or not, they could not simply spurn her. They even hired a porter to carry an A-frame piled high with all sizes of bundles, stuffed with grain and red pepper powder. Grandmother went so far as to accompany us, decked out in her finest dress.

The twenty ri to Gaeseong seemed unimaginably far. We crossed fields and climbed hills. Everywhere that a field and hill met was a village, some bigger than Bakjeok Hamlet and others smaller, but the way they sat in their surroundings was familiar, as was the way the houses looked. I had accepted villages as part of a larger natural order. The fourth and final hill, Wardrobe Rocks Hill, was particularly steep, or so I must have thought because my legs hurt so much by that point. Mother told me to keep going. Songdo lay just beyond, she reassured me. I puffed. I huffed. Mother pushed me from behind. My mouth was parched with the exertion, but at long last I managed to scramble to the top.

And then a sight I'd never witnessed before spread beneath me: the Songdo I'd heard so much about. I let out a cry, awestruck at this beautiful city gleaming silver. Its roads and houses dazzled me. I later learned that all its large new buildings were built in granite. The sandy soil gave the city its characteristic rocks and roads of white. *So people live in places like this!* I gaped as I stared, enchanted by the artificial order and neatness.

Suddenly a blinding flash shot from a building straight into my eyes. The light was unlike any I'd seen before. There was no fire, but it was more intense than any flame. I clung to my mother in fear. She told me to stop being

silly, that it was just the sun reflecting on a glass window.
I could make out that a sunbeam was hitting something
and giving off a ray, but I didn't understand what she
meant by 'glass window'. She then explained to me that
in big cities like Songdo and Seoul everybody used glass
for house windows.

In Bakjeok Hamlet, too, we had something made of glass.
The grown-ups called it a sake bottle. It was placed under
the veranda and stored kerosene poured from a canister.
People live in houses with windows of glass! I was amazed,
but at least half my fascination when I gazed on Songdo was
anxiety. I sensed I was standing not so much on Wardrobe
Rocks Hill as on the border of two totally different worlds.
I felt inexorably drawn to this unknown realm but at the
same time I wanted to take a few steps back.

I could almost hear my heart pound. An instinctive fear
gnawed at me—I was at a crossroads, about to turn from
the easy life I had known onto a path of challenge.

The descent wasn't hard. Halfway down we passed a
cluster of huge hexagonal rocks that had given the hill its
name. Sweet spring water gushed forth among them, and
they really did look like a slew of wardrobes scattered about.
I sat on one that resembled a long, long money chest and
quenched my thirst.

Finally, we marched into Songdo. We crossed railway
tracks and passed alleys flanked by trim houses with tile
roofs. Eventually we turned onto a main thoroughfare of
packed earth, lined with two- and three-storey homes with
glass windows. Songdo was filled with things I'd never seen
before, but Mother's attitude made me feel like I shouldn't
cower or gawk.

Mother's confidence as she strode along struck me as
slightly unnatural, even if I couldn't explain why. She
seemed to be setting an example for me. All the girls had

short haircuts that revealed the pale backs of their heads. I felt a newfound respect for my mother. Some older girls did have long braids tied off with a ribbon, but not a single girl wore the tiny braids I sported in the village.

Finally we reached Gaeseong Station. It was magnificent, and people were bustling about inside. What would I do if I lost sight of the grown-ups? I was terrified. I'd never imagined such a possibility before and that made my fear all the more vivid. I clutched tightly at Mother's skirt, as she piled up our bundles near the gate and went to buy tickets. We showed them to an inspector and went out to the platform, where I saw a gigantic ladder suspended in mid-air. Mother called it an overpass, but even then, she made sure to boast that it was nothing in comparison to the one at Seoul Station, which was much bigger and more crowded.

We had an arduous trek, laden as we were. But when a train pulled in Mother began to run, bundles in her hands and on her head, followed by Grandmother, who had bought a platform ticket so she could see us off. I darted after them, bundles in my hands too. Other passengers joined in the mad dash. I sprinted with all the speed I could muster and boarded amidst all the confusion. The train made me think of a huge snake with glass windows. Grandmother helped us hoist our bundles on the rack above and went back out alone.

She then stood on the other side of the window where I sat. She was saying something, but I couldn't make out her words. Of all those seeing off families and friends, Grandmother looked smallest and shabbiest, but that very shabbiness drew me to her. How amazing glass was! I could gaze clearly at her as her eyes welled with tears. I wanted her to gather me in her arms, so I could weep with her and have her caress me and murmur, 'My poor baby.'

I pressed against the window, squishing my face against it as if against a sheet of ice, but couldn't get any closer.

The train shrieked out a piercing, melancholy whistle and then began to chug away. Those saying goodbye to loved ones walked alongside until they gradually disappeared from view. I couldn't see whether Grandmother had followed the train or just stood there. My tears poured forth in a torrent. I'd often sobbed loudly without crying, but I'd never wept silently when so many tears flowed. The heartbreak I felt was unbearable.

Finally we arrived in Seoul. Mother and I, with all our bundles, lagged at the tail of the crowd. Panting, we climbed a pedestrian overbridge that was indeed several times bigger and busier than Gaeseong's. Other people's loads were much lighter than ours and they could hand them to porters in navy blue uniforms and red caps. Mother, however, flailed about nightmarishly, struggling under the weight of our packages. A long, long time seemed to pass before we exited the ticket gate and reached the plaza in front of the station. Right in the centre of it, Mother shed her burden, the way she might pour out buckets of water, and plopped down in a heap. I was so overwhelmed by the crowds passing around us that it didn't even register with me that we'd arrived in Seoul at last.

A-frame carriers in tattered dirty clothes rushed to us, like a band of beggars, competing noisily to carry our bundles. Some tried to lift them away unasked. When it dawned on me we could hire a porter as we'd done from Bakjeok Hamlet to Gaeseong, I felt a semblance of hope return. But Mother shook them all off, saying we'd take a streetcar.

A tram was running through the street. It was blue, shorter than a train carriage, and looked as if it had horns stretching from its back up to lines in the air. When I saw sparks leap between its horns and the lines, my curiosity turned into fear. Mother stayed sprawled on the ground, and the porters who had scattered approached again, one by one.

Mother chose a porter and began bargaining, but the criteria she used to pick one were beyond me. She pointed across the street with her chin. How much to go over there, to the other side of Seodaemun? The carrier quoted a price. Mother refused. She began pulling down the bundles he'd placed on his A-frame. How much did she have in mind, then? After a long bout of haggling, mother and daughter were at last liberated from their burden. We walked on ahead in front of him.

We passed a crowded street, dirty and noisy. Its dust and grime were reflected in the clothes of the people who walked along it. After crossing a big intersection through which streetcars travelled, pedestrians thinned out and the road began to look more like the one I'd seen in Gaeseong. Further ahead loomed a large gate that blocked the street.

'That's Independence Gate,' explained Mother. The A-frame carrier, trailing behind, asked breathlessly whether we'd arrived yet.

'Just a little further.' A wheedling smile flickered on my mother's face.

'How far is "a little further"?'

'Over there, Hyeonjeo-dong.'

Before she finished her sentence, he stopped in his tracks. His eyes bulged in anger. Was this some kind of joke? Who'd go all the way up that hill for the amount of money she'd offered? Mother held her ground, retorting with a question of her own: why would she pay several times more than the tram fare, instead of riding in comfort if her destination was in the flats of Seoul? She coaxed him onward, saying she was considering adding a tip so he could buy some rice wine. He grumbled, cursing his luck for the day, but followed anyway. Once the name 'Hyeonjeo-dong' had come out of my mother's mouth, though, he became noticeably rude. It was all too clear that he looked down on us. Where on earth was Hyeonjeo-dong to make him behave as he did? My spirits sank at the change in his attitude.

The double streetcar tracks that had accompanied our journey came to an end. Mother entered an alley that soon turned into a series of precipitous steps lined by houses. It was a strange neighbourhood. The houses clustered together on a steep hill and looked ready to tumble down its side at any moment. The houses had simple plank gates, but you could see everything that went on inside them. Drainage grooves running along the steps brimmed with a fetid mix of cabbage leaves, rice grains, and urine.

We struggled to the top of one hill without stopping, but the neighbourhood continued. On we went, following an alley that twisted and turned, barely wide enough for two people to pass, until we came to steps even steeper and less regular than those we'd climbed below. Finally, about halfway up, my mother stopped in front of a thatched house, one of the few even in this poor neighbourhood. But that house wasn't ours, either. Mother was merely renting a room next to its gate.

The room was cramped and gloomy and had a tiny attached veranda. The only furniture was a chest of drawers, papered in a brightly coloured pattern of deer, turtles, and the so-called 'herb of eternal youth'.

Since the women in my family didn't have to work in the fields, they must have had time to burnish our furniture, for the chests that lined one side of every room in our house gleamed. Grandmother had brought a three-tiered chest with her when she got married. Although some nickel hinges were missing from its doors and they didn't open properly, the wood of the chest had a deep, subtle sheen. In the corner of one room, an opaque blue-grey vinegar jar with a long neck and fat tummy sat beside the wardrobe. For years vinegar had been stored in it, its acidity staining the jar naturally. I found the jar very beautiful. It struck me as mystical, just like the shrine to the household spirit in the yard. As far as I could tell, vinegar was made by pouring leftover liquor or rice wine into the jar. Sometimes small moths flew out. My grandmother considered that jar precious, saying our vinegar was the best in the village. If anyone asked for some, she refused, saying she was afraid her recipe might be stolen. She issued this pronouncement with such solemnity that she didn't sound stingy, and I felt a mysterious power in her words.

Heartbreaking images of that long-necked jar, the wardrobe of fine-grained wood, and the harmony they created within the room came to me. It was a scene of paradise lost. My own sense of beauty had developed under the influence of aesthetics handed down for centuries. The chest that confronted me here, with its hasty paper job and tacky colours, insulted my eyes.

Translated from the Korean by Stephen Epstein and Yu Young-nan

Mohd Affandi Hassan

Mohd Affandi Hassan has proposed the analytical and theoretical framework called Persuratan Baru, literally 'new letters', or Genuine Literature. This should not be seen as a 'bandwagon' post-colonial attempt to replace Western values with local creative ones, but rather an initiative to bring back the Islamic literary tradition to which the region was heir, which was elbowed out under Western colonialism in the nineteenth century.

Persuratan Baru differentiates between story-making (which it sees as Western-derived) and discourse-elucidating or knowledge-disseminating (which it sees as characteristically Islamic). Somewhat controversially, such writers are no longer interested in filling up the narrative space of a text with narrative components but rather with what Hassan calls discourse components, with the focus on producing a text which educates the reader. The story 'Still Learning' (Masih Murid Lagi) is an example of Persuratan Baru.

Still Learning

At first he was angry when he saw his daughter's marks were so low, but when she told him that her teacher had explained that all her answers were correct, only that they were exactly the same as the ones in the textbook, and so showed no original thought, he laughed out loud. The teacher's action was really funny.

'Your teacher said you didn't think, and only copied from the textbook?' he asked his daughter.

'Yes, Father. She said my answers were exactly the same as in the textbook, and so I shouldn't get full marks, some marks had to be taken away because I was accused of memorising the answers. Teacher said I don't know how to think.'

He laughed again.

'You think your teacher's right?' He was testing his daughter's intelligence.

'I don't agree with her, but I'm only a student, I can't object. The principal will punish me if I protest,' said his daughter.

'So you think your teacher's and principal's actions are right?'

'I believe they are confused,' said his daughter firmly.

'Why? Confused how?'

'I followed what the examiner wanted, answered what was asked, and didn't give opinions,' said his daughter, boldly.

'But the Minister of Education and our country's intellectuals have said that nowadays schoolchildren aren't able to think, they only know how to copy. They follow exactly what is in the textbooks, and they're not able to argue their viewpoints. What do you say to that?'

'I agree, Father. But it's not fair to expect Form 4 or Form 5 students to think like university lecturers who write academic papers. We only write exam answers, we're not asked to give opinions.'

He smiled, apparently pleased.

'So you're not going to accept the marks you've been awarded?'

'No. All my answers were correct. I should have got an A+, not just a C.'

'Good. We'll meet with your teacher, and your principal too. I think they're both confused, or are taking this too lightly. They're the ones who aren't thinking.'

At the meeting, the principal excused herself because she had some other important work to do.

'If you're busy, we can discuss this another time.'

'The teacher can help clarify your confusion,' the principal replied.

'This is no longer an issue about the teacher, but a matter of principle. A matter of conceptual understanding. It's about knowledge.'

'I'm sorry, I'm extremely busy.'

'I'm busy too, madam. I took leave today when I was told that you would be available, but now you say you are not. I can cancel today's meeting, but you'll have to decide when you can be here to discuss this matter seriously. If we only think about how busy we are, we'll never get anywhere. You have to make yourself available to discuss this. It's important.'

'Very well then, let's meet another time.'

The principal would not budge, would not negotiate, and rushed off to parts unknown.

'I'm sorry, sir. Can't the two of us discuss this?' the teacher asked.

'You don't understand. I wanted the principal to be here, so she would realise that a big mistake has been made. I want to know where she stands on this. If she's not here, this matter will not be resolved.'

'I'm sorry.'

It was the rudest apology he had ever received. Not the history teacher's, but the principal's. He'd come to the school after the principal herself had told him that she would like to be present at the discussion. Now she had simply rushed off. He believed she had deliberately left to avoid facing facts. As a father, he wanted to know why it was that, according to the new ruling in the school system, a student wasn't able to get an A+. By what ruling? That was what he wanted to know for sure. He didn't want to involve the Ministry of

Education, not yet. He wanted to hear the teacher's and the principal's point of view and reasons.

They met again nearly a month later, after repeated requests.

'All right, here's my problem. My daughter's answers in the test were all correct, exactly as stated in the history book, the textbook. My question is: why were her marks lowered?'

The history teacher blinked at the principal, as if hoping to be rescued.

'This was all the result of my own directive, sir,' the principal said proudly. 'We received instructions from the Ministry that students are to be tested on their intelligence and their critical thinking, not on their ability to memorise or rewrite what is in the textbooks or in any book they read, or on their ability to reproduce whatever the teacher said in class. They have to show that they can think. Your daughter is very good at memorising, but hasn't demonstrated her ability to think. That is why she only got a C. The ones who qualify for an A or A+ are the ones who can show they can think. I hope you are satisfied with this explanation and understand now how we work.'

'How many actually got A and above?'

'How many?' the principal asked the teacher.

'None. The highest was a C. Your daughter got the highest mark.'

He smiled.

'A C is not the highest grade.'

'I meant the highest in that particular test,' the teacher protested.

The teacher and the principal became uncomfortable as they saw their visitor was still smiling.

'This is quite difficult. If anyone had got an A or above, we could discuss how you evaluated them. Now this is still unclear. Can you clarify how you grade them, or what you mean by "thinking"?'

The principal answered quickly:

'We were told by the Ministry of Education that if Malaysia wants to develop, our children must be able to think, not just copy. At the moment, textbooks are written not to help thinking, but to encourage memorising. We must act quickly and precisely to fulfill the Ministry's directive, and this is why in the recent tests, we have tried to implement this ruling.'

He felt sorry for the principal, who had explained at length, but had no substance to her explanation. Evidently the principal had no idea at all about the concept of thinking in education. This innovation that she wanted to introduce had caused so much confusion. It was the smart students who ended up being punished because of this confusion and the fact that the teachers themselves had only a superficial understanding of the concept.

'What you said was a directive was actually not a directive, merely an opinion. And it was aimed at university students, not junior secondary school students. Secondary school children should not be burdened with the task of thinking. It's enough for them to be exposed, through education, to ways of thinking in general, in order to create a love of knowledge and an admiration for the achievements of intellectuals. This isn't necessary for all subjects. In mathematics, there is no need to involve critical thinking, students only need to develop their mathematical skills. This doesn't mean that there are no instances of thinking in mathematics. I mean, if the maths teacher is smart, she can show her students how numbers, lines, space, density, weight and so on can be turned into formulae because all of God's creations have their specific measurements. If the teacher knows the history of mathematics, she can, for example, tell how Muslim mathematicians were interested in astrology, mathematics, and music. Al-Farabi was a mathematician, a scientist, a philosopher, a musician, and a maker of musical instruments as well. The teacher can tell the students how the wise Al-Farabi created the musical instrument known as the kanun based on mathematical knowledge. Why was there a need for this musical instrument to be created? It is because in the human soul there is an artistic side, an aesthetic side. The eighty-one stringed instrument created by Al-Farabi, the kanun, served as a channel for one of the aesthetic sides, that is, the appreciation of the beauty of sound. And what a beautiful sound it produces. Have you heard the sound of the kanun?'

Both teachers smiled, uncertain, and slightly embarrassed. They had never heard the name of the instrument, let alone heard it played.

'We have to produce our own Al-Farabi, but not by punishing our children with our own confusion. Form 4 or Form 5 students don't need to think like university students. It's not their job to think. They simply need to be trained to think. How? By telling them stories such as the one about Al-Farabi, so that their hearts will be attracted to the world of mathematics, which in turn will lead them to want to create something new. Not all examination answers require critical thinking. In the subject of history, it is sufficient for Form 4 or Form 5 students to know historical facts. Give them marks for that, not for debating why Tun Perak prevented his family from becoming palace officers, or defied the king's command to kill Hang Tuah. That would be the work of a scholar, not a school child. If you want to teach learners how to think, do it through lessons in language, literature, art, or art education. Art education is the best place to learn to think creatively, but in our country this is not done. Why did we throw out something beautiful from our education system? When someone uses colour and makes lines on a piece of paper, he is able to perceive immediately the change in his thinking. If he chooses a colour, and decides to draw a particular type of line rather than another one, he is able to see how his decision helps determine the end product. That's what thinking is. As children grow older, and are able to understand how language shapes their writing, we can teach them to appreciate the beauty of language. Beautiful language is not just flowery language, with unclear metaphors and wild similes. One such example is: "Dia tersenyum seperti jubur ayam lepas berak", "his smile is like a chicken's arse after it shits". Have you heard of this simile? The person who wrote it has been given an award, but here it's clearly vulgar language being promoted, not beautiful language. We must teach our students to learn about the beauty of language, not its vulgarity. Make them learn that choice of words, paragraph flow, sentence construction, and so on and so forth, will influence the quality of their writing. This is training in thinking. It has to be linked to how children structure their thinking. They must have logic. This is where mathematics is important. And this is why in the development of human civilisation, mathematics and language play important roles as the basis for the establishment of a civilisation. Our children must be taught to master the best forms of language, and to acquire the highest skills in mathematics. Unfortunately, we have neglected these two aspects. Which is why Malay children especially are very backward in their thinking. Language is beautiful, mathematics is beautiful, thus the two must be mastered together, or at the very least, one of them must be mastered. What do we do? End up being weak in both. And now we talk of our children having to learn to think, without providing them with a sound foundation. What are we doing really? Merely ruining our own children. We teach them to hate learning when we should be teaching them to love knowledge. How can they love knowledge if intelligent children are punished? They answer the questions correctly, but the marks are lowered. What exactly are we doing, if this is how our teachers behave?'

The principal's face flushed. Her lips moved, as if wanting to say something, but her throat felt too parched to speak. The history teacher bowed her head, silent, not even daring to look up.

'What is your opinion, Madam Principal? Am I wrong, or am I right? I would like to hear your opinion,' he said, challenging her.

'Sir, you're not taking our increasing workload into account. We're teaching your daughter as best we can, and yet you're criticising us,' Madam Principal replied.

He felt like shouting at her.

'I asked for your opinion, not excuses . . .'

'We've done our best for your daughter. If she isn't able to think, what more can we do? We work as directed by the Ministry, not as directed by the parents . . .'

He shook his head, perplexed by the principal's words.

'I will try to follow your advice,' said the history teacher.

'We have official directives. We only follow official directives. I don't believe we need to discuss this any further. Your daughter's marks will not be changed . . .'

'I will report our discussion to the Minister of Education himself,' he said, firmly.

The principal was shocked. Her face was pale, her lips trembling.

'Don't do that, sir. Don't report it to the Ministry. Let's settle this amongst us. Can you mark this gentleman's daughter's exam paper again?'

'No need, madam. I will not allow that. The paper is important as documented evidence when I discuss this with the Minister of Education.'

The principal was on the verge of tears, her face extremely pale. The father, who was starting to feel sorry for the frightened principal, excused himself and left.

He didn't know what the principal and the teacher discussed, but he was surprised to see the teacher running to his car.

'Are you really going to take this up with the Ministry?'

'Yes. Why do you ask?'

'Please don't, sir. The principal hasn't got her promotion yet. If you report this, maybe she won't be promoted.'

'Why not? She has followed the Ministry's directive. She won't be punished for following orders . . .'

'It's not like that, sir. We've done all this on our own initiative, to show some proactivity on our part. I hope you understand.'

He stared in surprise at the frightened woman.

'Subhan'Allah, you've been playing with an educational principle? If you haven't seen the light yet, don't do it. This is not proactivity, but stupidity. Don't you see that?'

'Sorry, sir. The principal is in tears. She's afraid that her promotion won't be approved. *Please don't make trouble for us, sir.*'

He stared pityingly at the teacher, then got into his car.

'Tell the principal I won't take this to the Ministry,' he said, with a smile.

'Thank you, sir,' the teacher replied, with a nervous giggle, and a quiver in her voice.

Translated from the Malay by Washima Che Dan

Ananda Devi

Ananda Devi was born in Mauritius, of Indian ancestry. She is the author of nine novels, three volumes of short stories and one of poetry. One of her recent novels, *Ève de ses décombres* (Gallimard, 2006), won the Prix RFO and the Prix des Cinq Continents de la Francophonie, two major literary prizes for writers in the French language. Her work is highly poetic and often sombre, and incorporates both Mauritian Creole and Hindi. Devi lives in Switzerland.

The text published here is an extract from the novel *Pagli* (Gallimard, 2001).

Gato lamarye

Backwards. A woman clattering saucepans. The noise from the kitchens is too deafening. Actually, it's me. I'm the one who lets the rice burn because I like that smell of bitterness, the one who's not allowed the kokorni after I've prepared the ghee, the one who in the middle of the silent afternoon drops the heavy cast iron pots for the sheer pleasure of hearing the metal thunderstorm that rolls and crashes for a long time in the still air and seeing the little cracks spread across the cement floor that's always cold under my bare feet. But none of these disasters reveals what's going on inside me, that my heart is cold too, and lonely, that lightning is still ready to leap from my belly. I'm not Pagli, the madwoman, yet, but my dreams already inhabit me.

I know I'm lucky to live in a painted concrete house like a pink and white wedding cake. But I hated it on sight and all this fancy icing, this gato lamarye, makes me feel sick. The floor's so well waxed that you don't walk on it, you skate. The glass-fronted cupboard in the parlour holds knick-knacks that look like the people who live in the house, frozen in the complete unfeelingness of their bodies. I detest this mildewy life that's waiting for me. There are plastic lace doilies lying on the table in the middle of the parlour and protecting the backs of the armchairs as well, even if no one sits there. The cushions, in covers hand-knitted by the women of the household, have never lost their shape. Life goes on outside and in the outdoor kitchen, where gossip and rumours are free to spread with the cooking smoke. That's where people come together and share the daily ritual of saying nasty things about other people, ruining and destroying them with just a word and a tight little smile. This is the place I come to, the stranger, the rain-soaked new bride.

I never got used to it. So clean on the outside, and on the inside, so many layers of dust. I could hear them, outside the house, over the racket made by the water barrels and the balie koko scraping over the stones. Their tongues were constantly wagging. Zot lalang pa aret bate. And their charity stopped at the front door.

I found this out when I tried to offer a beggar woman something more than cold, empty, meaningless gestures.

She came every afternoon and stood in front of the entrance. She didn't ask for anything. She sat down on the ground and scratched at the scabs on her skin to make them bleed. She watched the blood trickling down as if it wasn't hers. The women of the household would give her a few coins and some food in an old tin bowl. One day when I was on my own, I went out and tried to talk to her. She just signed to me that she was hungry. I took her into the house.

She followed me inside obediently, into the parlour. She wanted to sit on the floor but I settled her in an armchair. She stroked the red velvet with delight, and laughed out loud to see the fluffy dog nodding its head up and down on a dresser. The house seemed disturbed by this laughter, in sharp contrast to the usual muted stuffiness of women's voices.

I served her food and drink in the household's best china. I poured her some whisky in the glass used by the head of the family. I took a brocade sari from my wardrobe and draped it over her thin shoulders, as if she was the dulinn, the new bride. Transformed, she watched me moving about. She was brightening little by little, her face was soft, its drawn lines smoothing out, she began to smile a womanly smile, stroking the fabric, almost too luxurious. Even the dirt encrusted on her body seemed beautiful to me.

At one point, she brushed her hand lightly over my face and put her black thumb on my forehead, between my eyebrows, just where the missing married woman's tikka should have been. Tonn marye ek lamor, she told me gravely. That didn't frighten me. I'd rather be married to death than to someone who isn't alive.

When the others came back, she was afraid and huddled in my arms. She smelled of filth and refuse, but her trembling, defeated body moved me. I held her close as if she was my child. I could feel her heart beat, then clench and shrink. She was far more alive than the stares of astonishment and disgust trained on us.

They called her an untouchable. They made her leave, taking care not to brush against her, flapping their hands wildly as if shooing away a dog. She tore herself from my arms and fled. I saw her stagger out of the house, fall, then hurry away, moaning. She trailed my sari behind her like a veil. It was collecting dust from the roadway, becoming heavy with mud and life.

She disappeared. But she was free.

Then the women came back with rubber gloves, detergent and sticks of incense. They threw into the garbage everything she'd touched, scrubbed the rest, perfumed and purified the rooms. In the end there wasn't any taint of that poor starving woman left, not a single trace of her passing. The house had its glazed appearance again.

Then, and only then, did they turn to me. Their expressions were as corrosive as the bleach they'd poured everywhere. That's when I saw the name they've given me forming for the first time on their lips, and their insect thoughts coming to life and running over my body. 'What kind of creature is this that we've taken into our household?' they murmured. I wasn't just different. I'd become dangerous.

And always will be.

It doesn't much matter to me. I know I'm waiting. They talk about me as if I wasn't there. They've deleted me from what they take to be reality, which is really nothing more than the absence of life. But that look and that silence have been in me for a long time, ever since the Ceremony overwhelmed me with blackness. Or rather, the thing before the Ceremony. I'm here like an unfilled space waiting for the light.

Ter ruz

The evenings fall like a guillotine on the wedding cake house. Life has not the slightest interest for me. The greyness of grubby virtues surrounds me, a thick dark sleep into which they sink as if into a dung heap. I'm a thorn in their side. When they look at me they're speechless with exasperation. Nobody likes me and the feeling is mutual.

Outside, the noises continue. The land trembles as evening crouches over it. Then it starts to speak to me, to open me. No one else listens to it, but I sit by my window and drink it in deep through my nose. I know I must be red inside, all my tubes lined with red dust. But as time passes my senses stop registering ordinary things and only hear stories of insects and dust and sediment, and I go far far away because this volcanic land is just like me. Born of earthquakes, it lies in endless expectation of more eruptions. Perhaps one of them will take it back to its origins in fire and sulphur, outside of time.

I'm out of step. Half my life happens outside me. I don't know where I'm going. Or rather, I no longer know where I am when I come back, because I've been standing still and the rest of the world has gone on with their lives.

I was like this even as a child. I ran away from home and from school to lose myself in the cane fields. When I went home for the evening meal, I realised I hadn't eaten anything all day. Swallowed nothing but my saliva and the brown air of a country summer, because I'd spent the day running through the fields chasing after the call of a turtledove or the green flash of a parakeet I'd glimpsed between the leaves, I'd baked in the heat, stretched out on the big blue stones dug out of the fields, I'd whirled myself dizzy, listening to the clacking sound of the hoes against the cane stalks, I'd drunk deep of the water of greenness around me and life had flowed through me as if into a great clear vase.

That was enough for me. My slenderness allowed me to slip between people's watchful looks and lose myself, become invisible. It was a kind of happiness. But it didn't last. I knew I was destined for something else, because the old tattooed woman taken in by my parents had already told me so many times the story of my birth.

She told me my mother had been in so much pain that her heart had stopped at the exact moment that her body freed itself from me. The women had put me to one side on the bed while they took care of her. They had dragged her forcibly back into life.

Her eyes opened and her body began to tremble with rage that she had survived. And I must have realised then that I'd been abandoned. 'That's her forgetfulness that hurts you, that's her dead heart that haunts you,' the old lady told me as she held me between her legs, with me sitting on the ground and her on a little stool, pulling a fine-toothed comb through my hair.

My parents did their duty by me. Birthing me, growing me and losing me. They were people who needed all their energy just to survive. Their daughter's fate was of no interest to them except when her first blood flowed. The steps were clearly marked, planned well in advance. They didn't notice the emptiness in my eyes, that deepened with every lurch, every dislocation of my bones. They didn't know I had a heart and a body I was trying to understand. They weren't able to recognise the exact moment the cataclysm happened. I grew up alone, talking only to the tattooed woman about the terror I glimpsed inside myself, and then not talking at all any more, from that moment when, at the age of thirteen, I encountered darkness. 'There is still much pain in store for you,' she would say, 'it is written on your forehead and the palms of your hands.' And I would see that ocean of suffering reflected on her face and wonder what use it was to be born a woman if your destiny was written in letters of blood. I thought it was normal, in the end, when I was married, to come to this place that was the colour of my destiny.

Here, because I have no one any more and because the shadows surround me, I just listen. The wind, the birds, the earth, time passing. The dense and dangerous writing of this book. I am laden with memories not my own, waiting to live.

Terre Rouge is weighed down with stories. In its furious air there lurk endless days of blazing sun when people are driven mad by the brightness and filled with murderous urges. There are stories of seasons of unending rain when the mud rises up and buries the houses, cloaking them in crimson, and the villagers must dig holes through the coating to breathe and to look outside. Stories about slaves who died in particular places marked by their presence ever after and coloured by tears. About indentured labourers who spent their lives in search of something they could never find: rest. And this redness, says the earth, comes from all these unforgiven sacrifices. It will not so easily forget its history, the crimes that were its beginning and its end, the suffering that flowed directly into the soil and lodged itself inside the pockets of lava waiting to spurt forth again. And as long as people do not understand and accept this history, as long as they believe that this suffering keeps them apart instead of bringing them together because it was their meeting point, the lava will continue to boil and roar.

I don't know whether she is lying to me. Her stories seem to be made from a tissue of half-truths that enfold me and make me feel I belong to a different order. But at the same time it's as if they're leading me even further away from ordinary life, the life I am still condemned to live. This slipping away is dangerous. I don't listen to anything any more except the water on the tin roof of the hen house, a drumming that I find joyful in a different way from the endless Indian songs belching out of the transistor.

The world has so much to say. I feel so alone, by the window in the evenings, closely watching its changing moods. Because there's no one around me or behind me, no ordinary, reassuring presence that might have given me a sense of something shared, scarcely even the touch of familiar bodies, the brushing past of friends accustomed to one another's smells. The man given to me by the Ceremony is gone before he even got here.

At least, I did feel alone until I heard someone else's breathing, someone else's voice, and with the rising of the moon saw someone else's gaze filled with recognition.

You.

I knew you before I saw you. When I met you it was like a dazzlement beyond meaning. I felt you in my breasts before I knew who you were. They hardened suddenly and ached, as if the milk were coming in after giving birth. My eyes closed.

The wedding cake house collapses into its own insignificance. I am coming to life.

A voice calls me Pagli. Over and over again, as if to bring me back into line.

But you, you gave me a different name. Different names, several of them, a new one every time, depending on our mood, what I looked like, your laughter. Names of rain, of trees, of songs, names that spoke of rituals and miracles. Names of innocence and despair, cruel names, fragile names that crumbled into dust as soon as they were said.

I cannot hear them any more. I will not speak them. I will not think again of loss.

Pagli. Two syllables clinging to me. Two smooth swallow's wings wrapped around me. Two separated selves, one given over to love, the other feeding its fury. I pass from one to the other, up on the high wire without a net, then falling onto my blood-veined stones and losing myself completely in my own dismembered corpse. Pagli. That's who I am.

Translated from the French by Jean Anderson

Severino Salazar

Severino Salazar was born in 1947 in Tepetongo, in the Mexican State of Zacatecas. He was a professor of English at the Universidad Autónoma Metropolitana in Mexico City. He has published thirteen books (novels and collections of short stories) in Mexico, some of which have been translated into English and Italian. He died of cancer in 2005.

This story, 'Membrillos de terciopelo', is taken from his collection of short stories, *Mecanismos de luz y otras iluminaciones* (Ficticia, 2003).

Velvet Quinces

'When are you going to place your baby order?' they asked Tere.

'Can't you get it up, then?' they'd have asked Adrián.

'Those two keep clipping the stork's wings,' thought everyone in the village.

Tere and I have been friends forever, since we were little: we grew up together. We were neighbours. We had almost the same boyfriends; not at the same time, obviously. The same boys approached us, first one and then the other. But life blows hot and cold: she didn't like babies then, she didn't pick them up or cuddle them, she watched them from a distance as if they were strange little animals. Though later she would have given her life to have one.

Then she settled down with Adrián, who lived just opposite, and together they built a big, beautiful house on a piece of orchard his dad had given them, on the outskirts of the village and on the edge of a cliff, a few steps from the river. They knocked down a lot of fruit trees to build it. From their patio you could hear the water skipping over the stones or the wind whistling through the willows and poplars. He stopped depending on his father and set up his own butchery to sell meat, crackling and chorizo.

I used to ask myself: How many pigs has he killed in his life so far? Might his soul already have become like a pig's: selfish, wanting everything for itself, voracious, destructive, possessed by an insatiable hunger, holding on to all it can reach with its snout, interrupting the flow of everything, trapping all that it eats in its bottomless pork casing?

And once they were married, they wanted the most natural and simple thing in the world: to have a child. They loved each other very much. During the early years of their marriage you could see that they got on very well. You could sense from the outside that they were happy just the two of them and that they didn't need a little one. However, deep down inside, I think they imagined that what they still needed to be fully content was to see what it was like to be parents. Perhaps, as she got tired of hearing the same question over and over and as he surely got fed up with being the butt of his friends' occasional jokes, their minds became choked with smoke and who knows what else besides.

And they got it into their heads that they would do whatever it took to have that child. But God didn't want to give them one: He hadn't made the breath of life a part of their make-up, as our grandmas sometimes say. His will was that they should not have children. His will was, I believe, that they would have a different sort of marriage, just two people living together and that was that. But they saw things differently, they felt they should also behave the same way and have the same things as everyone else. But, I'll say it again: I believe that this was not God's will.

Or maybe they were terrified of exploring a new path on their own. Like going into a cave without knowing what's inside. Who knows what they were thinking, who knows what storm was in their minds? They threw their hearts into trying to bring about the miracle of parenthood. And they turned to all the methods within reach to make it happen, from the home remedies of midwives to treatments prescribed by medical specialists.

They were seen by an infinite number of doctors in Jerez, Zacatecas and even San Luis, but it all came to nothing. She used to tell me that she was ashamed of having to answer so many questions, of so much interrogation about her private life. Like how they do it and how often and at what time and for how long. And the doctors didn't come up with anything. Partial studies were carried out in a large number of hospitals and clinics, further and further away from home. They would leave the village in their van at odd times in the early morning; they would take with them samples of everything that oozed out of their bodies, or they would go without breakfast so that they could be analysed and studied. They spent so much money checking out his sperm and her eggs, if not in one city then in another, that their slaughtering business began to suffer.

And they would go back to their house—such a lovely one among the trees—feeling more miserable with each homecoming, with even less hope, but all the more keen to work so that they could keep being seen by doctors; and with a long list of recommendations as well: that they should now do it this way or that way. They even changed their diet and many of their habits. And at the same time, they learnt everything there was to know about the workings of the human body . . .

He had to lose a lot of weight: he ended up as thin as a beanpole, because a doctor told them that his seminal fluid was very thick. He didn't eat any of the meats or sausages that he sold. Somewhere else they were told that after doing it she had to remain practically standing on her head for quite some time so that the sperm didn't leak out, helping them to reach the egg.

How they struggled, how they threw their money away for nothing. All this time the village gossips amused themselves listening to and repeating all these new adventures—we'd never seen anything like it before in these parts when couples were trying to conceive. How could they not stop to think when they saw so many poor, filthy creatures all around them in the village, and there they were, throwing their earnings away, over and over again? But, according to my grandma, it takes all sorts.

Tere used to tell me: 'They assure us that only one of us has a problem. That we can't both have something wrong. That very soon they will cure us or they will reveal all. That soon we will have an answer. So we will finally be at peace, once and for all.' And my friend would go on turning the mincer handle round and round, filling metres and metres of pork gut with fragrant and delicious chorizo meat.

I thought to myself: Unfortunately, as soon as she has that child, we'll stop being friends. Not because I won't want to, but because for now she thinks of me as her equal. She would live in another world altogether once the little sprout she yearned for appeared.

Talking about this matter of procreation, I remember that my grandma put me in my place, as far as she was concerned, one afternoon when we were in our orchard. I remember that I was cutting off the ripest of the quinces and she was arranging them into a large basket. Because we'd had a lot of rain that summer, they had become so big and beautiful that it seemed like they were made of sweet-smelling, yellow velvet. They were so huge that I needed both hands to grab hold of them. The two of us were going to make that year's first pot of jam together.

And, out of the blue, she suddenly said: 'I find you a bit strange at the moment, my child, you seem sad to me, and I don't like it; I can almost guess word for word what is going through your mind. Excuse me for sticking my nose into something that doesn't concern me, though it does concern me, very much. But I'm doing it because I love you. And I don't want you to suffer, to think things that you shouldn't think, to sit there deluding yourself, to imagine Arabs in the attic, to misinterpret what you see before you. I want to help you to look at the world through the eyes of an old woman like me. God gives each one of us our destiny. And we have to accept His holy will. And not ask Him for any explanation, because if there is one, and there always is, we hardly ever find that we are capable of understanding it.'

'But I'm perfectly okay, Grandma, please, don't worry. I'm fine, really I am.' 'What are you talking about?' she answered. 'And don't tell me I've got it wrong. I know what thoughts go through your head when your brothers and sisters come with their children to visit us. That your eyes melt when you see them. That you don't know where to put them, how to please them, what to give them, which part of their little bodies to kiss and cuddle.' 'And is there something wrong with loving your nieces and nephews?' I asked her while I looked up at the sky, using my hook to bring down one of the quinces on the highest branches. 'No, there's nothing wrong with that, but the thing they leave you thinking is bad. And it's bad because it's not true.'

'But Grandma, what do they leave me thinking, what isn't true?' 'I'll tell you. You think: "If I love those children so much when they are only my nephews and nieces, what would this love, what would these feelings of tenderness be like if I were their mother? Could anything feel better than that? Maybe I'm missing out on a unique experience, something wonderful." All this business leaves you sad and thoughtful, my child; you can't hide it, especially not from me, an old woman who has seen so much.' 'Oh Grandma, you see too much,' I complained. 'I don't see too much at all; pay attention to what I say, I'm telling you.'

And when we were in the kitchen peeling the quinces and removing the cores for cooking, she carried on along the same lines: 'I've been wanting to tell you these things for days. And I couldn't think of a way to do it. But I'm glad I've finally told you; I feel relieved. Because you're watching from the sidelines, so to speak. And it's not the same thing to be the mother as to be the doting auntie. You only see them for short periods, when they're visiting and making merry, when they're clean and healthy. You don't know what it's like to struggle with them all day long. You're inventing feelings that don't exist, my girl. That's all. Believe me. Listen to what the old folk tell you.'

That night I slept badly, but later I felt some release from the everyday tensions of that glorious summer which passed through the village, showering its blessings on the orchards all the way along the river. The current made music as it crashed against the rocks; so did the wind as it swept through the branches of the black poplars and the elder trees. Grandma had given me a good fright in our orchard. I thought that she had other suspicions, that she actually wanted to talk to me about something else. That she had found me out. That afternoon, I felt dizzy for a moment and I thought I was going to topple off the wooden ladder I was using to reach the velvet quinces.

One morning, the summer suddenly vanished into thin air. And with the first cold autumn gusts, a woman from over in the barren and rocky farmlands of San Antonio and San Tadeo, those ranchos sinking in a sea of stones, arrived in the village, as if swept in by the wind. (They also say that the hearts of those people are rough, hard lumps of rock: that they heat up easily in the sun or cool down just as fast with the cold, but that they never burst.)

And like a bad smell, the news spread that the woman was sitting on a bench in the public garden with her four children, one no more than a baby, with a rough-looking young man wearing huaraches on his feet (she had just hooked up with him perfectly legally, in the Town Hall) standing smiling beside her, and that she was giving her children away, no strings attached, to anyone who wanted to finish raising them, so that later they could make themselves useful sowing seeds or running errands.

That same evening, she placed her offspring in the homes of four charitable families in this village; and all before they closed the registry office, where she was made to sign a few papers. After that she left with her coarse young man in a bus headed for Jerez, as casually as if she had just got rid of nothing more than a good crop of corn. Apparently off to make a new start, somewhere else, on life's mysterious journey.

Her cold heart wasn't moved in the slightest by the wailing of the two innocent older children who were begging her not to abandon them with people they didn't know, crying out that from now on they would be good. The younger ones didn't even realise what was happening to them.

Although we never heard anything more about that woman, we never forgot her. Because in a matter of hours on that first autumn evening, she had taught us a terrible lesson that would remain with us forever. She had left a permanent mark on our souls, as if engraved in fire, blood and tears. She had shown us just how far a human being burdened by desire, longing and endless searching can go. She had left us with our hearts all wrung out. If only ours, too, were made of stone . . .

My friend Tere and Adrián ended up with the smallest one. Still breastfeeding, poor little innocent baby, and not even three months old. The child turned out to be a girl. And so, that same evening, the terrible ordeal began for those two poor souls. Life for Tere and Adrián changed suddenly. It spilled over in all directions. Though I think they were better off. They were filled with new feelings, their house in the middle of the orchard was no longer the same house, fresh sounds and smells passed through it.

And I wonder, too, why so much longing? After all, why look for problems when there are none? If it can't be, then it can't be and that's all there is to it; why become obsessed and poison your life all the more when it's already such hard work? When there are already so many people in the world, when that's what there's too much of; so many little kids, why one more?

They should have gone along with God's will and been content that He hadn't yet saddled them with any burden. But they insisted so much that He seemed to laugh at them and say to Himself: That's what they want? Well, that's what they'll get. And he put a piece of live meat in their arms. A piece of meat that was suffering, that was unwell. As if to say: If they want to struggle, let them struggle. The poor creature was undernourished, and they had to get her some special glasses when she was five months old: she couldn't see, and as well as that, she was cross-eyed; when you talked to her she would stretch her tiny hands up into the air, trying to touch the words.

She had no strength in her hands or in her muscles. Although she was so small they put an A-shaped frame between her little legs because they twisted about in all directions. And how she cried, how she suffered, poor creature. They began to test her to see if she was mentally retarded.

And because they insisted, because they tempted fate, God gave them a heavier, more painful load to bear, I think, but I'm not going to say it. We have thoughts that must never be aired, must not come out as words.

From then on, the two of them left the village very early and drove off in their van towards Jerez; again they visited the doctors who had treated them earlier. They took the girl to be cured, to see other specialists and then to her analyses, her therapies and her exercises. They stopped worrying about themselves. Adrián began to put on weight again. Tere's face hardened and she even laughed in a different way. He didn't work for days on end, leaving his business in the hands of his assistants. Spending and spending, finishing off the little they had.

They became bitter and it made us sad as well to see their pain, to see them so impotent, not knowing what to do with that piece of meat that was so helpless, that suffered and twisted and turned in their arms, while they looked at each other in bewilderment as if asking themselves, what happened to us? The two whose job it was to demonstrate, to teach the rest of us in the village what it was like to be content, to be happy, just the pair of them, living together, uncovering and exploring the mysteries of a friendship with no responsibilities, no excuses, no restrictions.

Just as I had expected, my friend, Tere, wasn't the same person any more. Her mind was on different things. We no longer sat for hours chatting as we had done in the past. She would be just about to tell me something and she would stop in the middle, as if to say, without actually saying it: What would you know about such things, or why would you care about these matters? Or, I carry around thoughts that I can't get out, I feel things that I can't explain to you. She no longer had the face of a girl; even her voice was that of a woman.

And all because of that puzzle God had put into their arms so that they would wander here and there with it and find no peace—inside their minds and on the outside. She told me bitterly: 'They say I'm an empty egg, that I'm hollow.' And her voice came from a long way away, as if from deep inside her.

I spent every night of that season dreaming the same dream in different forms: I found myself in the orchard, picking and picking velvet quinces from the trees, in a bountiful, never-ending, obsessive harvest. And then peeling them and tearing out the heart of each one, that small, downy space, almost hollow, in the centre of the fruit where the seeds were nicely settled in and life and growth had begun. Throwing away those sacred places where life was sheltering, crouching down out of the way so as to be left to flourish. That space at the heart of the perfumed, tart flesh of the quince, empty and mysterious like a cathedral.

My grandma and I made more and more pots of jam. So many that the house wasn't big enough to fit the moulds, clay dishes, jars, jugs, pots and pans of jam that had now set. We were the victims of a sweet abundance of unnecessary proportions, which was overwhelming us. The smell of boiling jam and caramelising sugar wafted out of our house. And soon the river itself was a jam swamp, encircling the village.

Oh, dear God, why this need, this urgency to offer every last drop of our lives to someone else? Or are we, as Adrián says, that other, luminous part of a pig: generous, prolific, prosperous hoarders who store things up for the future, who, through strange processes in the darkness deep inside us, transform the filth into food, into sustenance?

We never stop learning and teaching other people. I have to leave the village soon. I'm pregnant. Before it begins to show and gossiping and scandal are set loose. Adrián tells me there are only three ways to get out of this predicament: first, for me to stay and live with the consequences; second, for me to go off on my own and get rid of it out there and then come back as if nothing has happened; or the last option, for the two of us to go off together and make a new life for ourselves far away from this village. But then I start to think about what my grandma sometimes says: What are we here for? Why did God bring us here? Not to keep fouling the minds of others, not to keep fouling the ground we walk on: knocking down trees to put up houses, throwing into the river anything we have left over.

I have barely a week to decide what to do. I am horrified to think that suddenly, without my wanting it, the destiny of many people is in my hands. And that time, in a woman's body, is relentless. As if God had also put a clock with a tightened spring deep inside us, a mechanism of light.

Translated from the Spanish by Frédéric-Yves Jeannet and Rolla Norrish

Claudine Jacques

Claudine Jacques was born in Belfort, France, in 1953, but has lived in New Caledonia for most of her adult life. Since co-founding the Association of New Caledonian Writers in 1997 she has devoted much of her time to writing, and has published three novels and five collections of short stories, as well as a number of works for children. Her writing presents a multicultural Pacific, as European, Kanak, Wallisian and other Pacific island characters encounter one another. This text is an extract from the novel *L'Homme-lézard* (The Lizard-Man) (HB, 2002).

The Lizard-Man

Some of my mates had to give up sculpture because they
just couldn't keep going, they had kids to feed.
Yann Conny, sculptor, Mwà Véé, 2001

The first fifty years of my life were dogged by poverty.
Rodin

Enok was feeling tired but much better when he was discharged from hospital at the end of the week. He moved in with Mandela who was still dossing down in the old woman's bedsit. It was a squalid ground-floor flat whose only window opened onto a closed courtyard. The dishwater from a nearby greasy spoon spewed out of dilapidated pipes and flooded a gutter which ran into the street. Things floating in the wastewater formed sticky piles on the ground where they slowly decomposed. Their putrid stench hung over the whole place. And you could hear everything: the clatter of saucepans, rubbish bins being moved, the boss shouting orders, the fawning giggles of tired waitresses.

Living there on her own, Mandela had been oblivious to all this: away early, home late, she hadn't noticed the constant racket, hadn't realised how sordid it all really was. Enok suffered through the smells and noises as he lay convalescing in this damp hell, staring at the tiny TV screen. Her brother's mute despair brought home to Mandela the harsh realities of the place. Her thoughts wandered back to the peacefulness of her tribal community up there in the north, to the breeze that swayed the palms and caressed her skin, to the smoky hut, the soft cooing of wood pigeons in the mist, the cry of the flying foxes, and their slow fluid flight in the mauve night sky. But they were just blurry, sketchy images that she quickly shook off, like a wild duck emerging from water. The golden mirages of the city were far more fascinating.

Enok had been surreptitiously watching his younger sister and was pained by the new differences between them: he had become as grey and dry as she was brown and luminous, as morose as she was cheerful.

As mute as she was eloquent.

But he would have to come clean about the city and its traps. The months of working for nothing. Selling off his sculptures, the good and the not-so-good, at cut-rate prices in the curio shops. The boozing just to keep going. The begging, stealing, gratuitous violence just to survive.

He put off the moment of truth by withdrawing into a stubborn silence that she still took for fatigue, but would soon no longer understand.

How could he tell her of his shattered dreams, his dashed hopes, his empty soul, his despair?

'I'm such a loser,' he sighed over and over again.

The meagre provisions they'd found in the old cousin's pantry didn't last long. The morning they ran out of food, Mandela turned towards Enok. She had just boiled the water for tea, reusing the same tea bag for the umpteenth time. There was no more sugar, just a scraping of niaouli honey left in the old whisky bottle. The look she gave her brother must have weighed on him more than the previous ones: Enok, sitting on the bed with his head in his hands, said awkwardly, 'You're going back to the tribe.' She got the message. These six little words weren't an order; they only meant that it was all too much for him, he couldn't do anything for her, worse still, he was giving up.

For the first time, Mandela dared to look straight at her brother; the expression on his face made all her childhood certainties disappear. Something had happened to him over the past two years but what could've been so serious that the big brother she worshipped, her beloved role model, was now just a shadow of his former self?

'I've changed, haven't I? I've been drinking a lot, you know, too much. It wasn't an accident that landed me in hospital, it was a drunken coma. Didn't need the doctors to tell me that.'

Lowering his voice even more, he confided:

'I nearly died, you know. The booze took all my strength.'

Then he was quiet. For the time being he preferred not to tell her about the street fights, the assaults, the times out biffing stones at cars. He'd been a spectator at first, then he'd joined in, practically a pro in causing trouble. Until the last incident when a baby had been seriously injured by the shards of glass from a shattered windscreen. All that just for some quick cash! It almost brought him to tears.

Mandela was not surprised, although something in Enok's

tone terrified her. A sense of urgency burned through her. There was a real reason for her to stay. He had cradled her as a child, taken her on the customary paths, taught her the names of the plants and the birds, treated her to grey prawns from the creeks and the first ripe fruits, protected her from the wind and rain without ever expecting more than a smile in return. Now it was her turn, quite simply, to step up and take care of their day-to-day needs. She was suddenly the big sister. That was how the world would carry on turning. She would have to drive out Enok's demons, forget her own dreams. Little-girl dreams after all, compared with her brother's ones!

She sat up straight.

'You've got to work things out. You're going back to your classes at art school.'

Enok's expression saddened.

'Mandy, naïve wee baby-girl, I can't do it any more.'

She was touched by his childhood nickname for her, and answered calmly:

'It's because your heart is lost somewhere deep inside you. You've got to find it again.'

He looked forlorn.

'I don't think I'll be able to . . .'

She cut him off:

'You don't need to worry about anything any more. I'm here.'

That night as she helped with the washing-up in the Chinese greasy spoon, Mandela kept one eye on the dishes, the other on the courtyard.

To get to the squat, you had to turn right at the tagged stone, go behind a huge African tulip tree, and follow a little dirt path lined with dust-covered pepper trees. Returning for the first time to the scene of the 'accident', as he preferred

to call it, Enok was on edge. He could see the small manioc
field down below where he had woken up. He could feel
a lump growing in the pit of his stomach, getting bigger
and bigger with every step he took, inflating like a rubber
ball. It wasn't the nakamal that was drawing him here, or
the faded memory of his fall, or the mates he'd run into at
the kava shack. He was on a sort of solitary pilgrimage,
retracing his steps on a soul-searching journey, to try and
understand his malaise but also—he really hoped—to make
amends and start over. He stopped near the guaiacum tree
and looked ahead in the direction of the blue tarpaulin still
flapping there in the breeze. Some children were chasing a
ball. Others were playing on a brand new slide.

A little girl, balancing on some pieces of chipboard put
down as flooring, yelled out:

'Granny, someone's coming.'

A young-looking woman with plaited hair rushed out of
the hut. She'd wrapped herself in a red and black Wallisian
manou, exposing the patched-up straps of a greyish bra. She
looked at Enok for a moment or two, trying to place him.

He walked towards her.

It was him all right.

She started laughing, her hand over her mouth. He could
see she was missing two teeth.

'Lord God Sésu! It's you the patient from the other
day?'

'Yes.'

'Malo.'

'Hello.'

'It's all right for you now? You leave hospital?' she asked
in her sing-song voice.

'Yes.'

She freed herself from the little girl who was clinging
to her manou.

'You go tell Lusia come quick.'

Then to Enok she said:

'The matua of me, he not here now.'

He didn't react. He'd guessed as much. She pointed at some plastic outdoor chairs and a table roughly assembled out of salvaged wooden pallets.

'Hau, come, you drink a tea.'

Enok slowly took a carved wooden comb out of his bag and put it on the edge of the table. He cleared his throat several times then, in a faint voice, launched into his thank you speech, looking down at his feet the whole time.

Tiarina, arms folded and deeply engrossed, wasn't listening, she was admiring the comb. She'd never seen one like it. The teeth were long, fine and even, the wood was shiny, the motif at the top was all curves and swirls, with satin-smooth hollows and polished contours. Enok went on to explain that he'd used the flecked texture of the blue wood to create this shell-shaped Venus comb, a real party piece. When he finished, she thanked him in turn, evoking Sésu, Malia the Blessed Virgin, and her duty to help her fellow man, then she grabbed the comb and planted it deftly above her heavy plait.

Lusia was coming.

When she arrived, the three of them were able to have a leisurely conversation that was above board, beyond reproach by others in the squat. So Enok was an artist, a carver, was he? He looked much better. His sister had arrived from the bush as well, she was called Mandela, a pretty Tahitian name, Lusia claimed. Enok let it slide. And she was working in town, in a Chinese greasy spoon. They were both looking for a place to live because the old woman, their cousin, was coming home soon. Tiarina came from the fénua, and over there in the homeland her husband couldn't find any more work; she had three children, the next one was due at the end of the month; Lusia, her best friend, was from the tribal community at Saint-Louis, had two girls and two boys, the ones running after the ball with her own sons.

An hour passed during which Enok was made to drink several cups of tea and eat his fill of thinly sliced fried yam spread with salted butter. Then he got up.

'I'll be on my way.'

'Fine,' the two women answered.

He grabbed his bag and patted the wavy-haired head of the little girl who had been quietly watching him. Tiarina and Lusia carried on eating and talking without paying him any more attention. This was serious business, organising the community bingo run by their women's group.

'So who the money go to?'

'This time, it's for the Belep Island woman.'

Lusia nodded, pityingly.

'Aouh! You know she. She need it real bad.'

Then she looked at the long, thin silhouette of Enok disappearing into the trees and murmured:

'Sure I seen him before, but where?'

Enok walked distractedly along the path to the nakamal. He realised he'd never seen the place sober and might have gone right past it if the giant clam shells on the ground and a rough inscription on a piece of corrugated iron hadn't reminded him where the entrance was.

A man wearing a manou was asleep in the shade of a fig tree. His scaly grey skin and skeletal thinness immediately marked him out as a hardened kava drinker. A van was delivering bags of roots that the boss, with the help of two young men, was storing away in the small windowless shed next to the main hut. There had, it seemed, been an attempt to do up, or at least organise, the site. Coconut tree trunks were being used as stools or bench seats around two distinct fireplaces, bamboo sticks had been shoved into the ground and decorated with fern masks to separate these new zones, someone had added stones from the river and carted in sand to try and make walkways.

It was all pretty slapdash.

Enok was pained by it, without knowing exactly why. Maybe he was more attached to the place than he'd thought!

He was about to leave when one of the young men recognised him and called out: 'Enok! Hey, man!' then came over to shake his hand. It was Lewis, nicknamed Porto after the birthmark staining his face.

'How's it going? Good to see ya. You been underground or what?'

'Trip,' he muttered with difficulty.

'I'm working here, at the nak. The brothers took me on because I don't drink their peppery poison. Brings me out in a rash. And then I swell up like a pufferfish. Not a pretty sight! Anyway, that's the job. Good timing, I wanted to talk to you about something serious.'

He lowered his voice:

'It's about your sister.'

Enok had been mindlessly scuffing the end of his jandal in the dirt but suddenly froze.

'I'm asking you for permission to talk to her. No hidden agenda, eh? Look, I'm not going to be a loser all my life, had a gutsful of underpaid odd jobs; I've got plans, I'm making good dough now and I'm gonna make even more.'

Enok didn't answer. He just gazed into the distance. Lewis insisted:

'I promise you I'll respect her. I'll never hurt her.'

He would have liked an answer straight away, some kind of consent or sign of approval, but at least Enok hadn't said no flat out. He went on, pointing at the boss of the nakamal:

'I work for him. We just got the goods in from Tanna. That's what I deal in, imports!'

He waved at the surroundings.

'As you can see, it's going really well. We're starting to get a damn good reputation. It's because of the roots. Awesome quality. And ya know, the kava here is strong stuff, believe you me! Come and see.'

Enok followed Lewis around the hut and into a poky little hovel, its corrugated iron walls white hot under the midday sun. Inside, men were filtering kava through a sieve into a big rubbish bin. Sweat was pouring off their shoulders, running down their shiny bare backs, soaking their soccer shorts, trickling down their thighs and calves.

An acrid, peppery odour mixed with the strong stench of the workers added to the clamminess of the place. The men didn't look up.

As he left, Enok noticed the coconut shell bowls drying on the thin grass and looked at them pensively.

Lewis misread him:

'Want a sel of kava?'

Enok gestured no and walked away.

He wasn't ready.

Translated from the French by Sarah Powell

Vladimir Voinovich

Vladimir Voinovich (b. 1932) is a well-known comic and satirical writer. His best-known work, referred to in this piece, is *The Life and Extraordinary Adventures of Private Ivan Chonkin*, set in the Red Army during World War II. Chonkin is now an important figure in Russian popular culture. Voinovich was ostracised by officialdom during the late 1970s and 80s and spent some time in Germany before returning to Russia in 1990. Several of his novels have been translated and he has won a number of prizes, such as the State Award of the Russian Federation (2000) and the Sakharov Award (2002).

This piece originally appeared in the *New Zealand Slavonic Journal* (2003) and is reprinted here by permission.

Stream of Consciousness

I've always wanted to master the stream-of-consciousness technique—it's a wonderful genre, and incredibly user-friendly! No need to think up a plot, draw your threads together or create believable characters. You just sit down and think—or better still, lie down and think. Especially when you have turned the TV on, and there's someone mumbling away, with images flickering across the screen, you're dropping off, your eyes start to close—that's when the stream of your consciousness starts to flow, carrying all sorts of flotsam and jetsam with it. It all gets mixed up in your mind—your impressions from the day's events, you remember something you did, or didn't do, one incomplete

thought is pushed out of the way by another one, still in
its infancy; a line, phrase or joke flashes through your mind,
you really should get up, switch on the light, put your
glasses on, grab a piece of paper and a pencil, but you don't
need paper, or a pencil, you've got your palm pilot—it's
easier to write on that, but you can't be bothered, I'll write
it down tomorrow, OK?—but I know already that by
morning it will all have blown away and evaporated. The
important thing isn't the existence of a thought, but its
birth in some sort of formulation in words—the formulation
disappears somewhere, and without it the thought isn't a
thought any more. You think about things eternal and
ephemeral, life, death, a war in progress somewhere or
other, and cities in ruins: Beirut, Kabul, Grozny. I had the
idea of offering to lease Grozny to Mosfilm Studios as a
joke, for shooting films about Stalingrad, but just as I was
thinking about that, the attack that destroyed the towers
of the World Trade Centre took place—and I didn't feel
like joking any more. Suicide terrorists who had learned
to fly had killed six thousand people, just like that. Was it
six or seven thousand? Somehow it seemed no one had got
around to doing an exact head count. We had a pilot in
1941, Captain Nikolai Gastello (or was he only a legend?),
who, with his bomber on fire, (supposedly) flew straight
into a column of German tanks, but he was going down
anyway, whereas these guys had deliberately sacrificed
themselves in a struggle for goodness knows what. In the
USSR we were taught from childhood that holding true to
your convictions is almost the supreme virtue, we were
taught to honour our heroes, particularly those willing to
sacrifice themselves. So are we supposed to respect this lot
as well? Yesterday's moral values belong to . . . yesterday
(excuse the tautology). As a godless crew ourselves, we used
to think that people who go to church, or to the mosque

or synagogue, were better and more humane than us, but now we realise that's not true, religion doesn't make people better, in some cases it infects them with worse hatred than you would find in any atheist. In fact I'm always wary of strongly religious people, particularly when they parade their beliefs by some externally visible feature, say by wearing an impractical item of clothing or letting their hair grow in some awkward way—turbans, beards, or the gabardine coats or side curls worn by orthodox Jews. The Communists were believers too—the only difference was that they believed not in God, but in His absence. I prefer the doubters. I'm a doubter myself. I hardly believe in anything. I don't believe in the proofs that God exists, nor yet in the proofs that He doesn't. There's nothing wrong with non-believers setting out those proofs, but the believers need to reflect on the depth of their faith if they can believe that God didn't want to reveal His secrets to us, but somehow made a mistake and revealed a few things after all. And in any case, are there any believers without doubts? Those who say of themselves that they have no doubts are lying—to themselves and to others. And anyone who says he never lies is lying as well. Everybody tells lies. Lying doesn't always mean being deceitful. There are such things as white lies. Politeness is a form of lying. The most common lie is 'How well you're looking!' In Russia doctors lie to their terminally ill patients, telling them they are going to get well. In the West they tell them the truth. When they told Borya Briger he was dying, he was about to pull out all the tubes they had stuck into him, then he thought better of it and set about drawing up his will. Just by the by, I believe he was a great artist. Perhaps he didn't have a lot of variety in his technique—he worked for many years in more or less the same style, but within the limits of that style he achieved perfection, there's something in his paintings which is the true stuff of art—real magic. But to come back to lying, I have just remembered: about thirty years ago a KGB investigator, while interrogating Professor Leonid Pinsky, tried to accuse him of dishonesty, and asked: 'Shouldn't an honest person always tell the truth?' 'Certainly not,' Leonid Efimovich answered, without hesitation: 'There was one man who told the truth, and the whole of mankind has been cursing his name for two thousand years.' Mankind curses Judas. But Peter also denied Christ, and so did the other disciples to some extent. When Christ was arrested in the Garden of Gethsemane they all ran away. Judas told the truth, and received his fee—thirty pieces of silver. These days he would write his memoirs and be paid a lot more. The genre of confessions and shocking revelations is right in fashion at the moment. Literature is probably the only area of human endeavour where the dilettante is more highly regarded than the professional. In the book market, it's as if costume jewellery was being sold from the same counter as real precious stones, and at the same price was even more popular than the real thing. In any area of activity, it would be ludicrous to hire a dilettante. If you can't dance you won't be taken on as a ballet soloist, and if you can't sing you're not going to become an opera star. But it's not like that in literature. A book by a famous tennis player or boxer will probably cost more than a book by a well-known writer—if only because no contemporary author is ever going to reach the same heights of fame as a leading sports performer. It's not just sportspeople, either. Monica Lewinsky became famous from one act of oral sex, and nothing else, and was then apparently paid a million dollars for her book (and yet what on earth would she have to write about???). Since the advent of universal literacy and access to culture, the demand for books hasn't been based on the interest of the material or on quality—the

devil only knows what makes them sell. Mass culture is a
sign of our times, and a mark of democracy. The masses
have become literate, and affluent enough to buy books
and go to concerts. And they force their taste down everyone
else's throat. I'm not interested in sport or in pop or rock
music, but nonetheless I know everything about Mike
Tyson, Madonna and Maradona. I know who Boris Becker
has been sleeping with, who he has divorced and who he's
going to marry next time round. I'm not interested in these
people, I don't want to know anything about them, but I
am force-fed this knowledge from the newspapers, magazines
and TV. If you really didn't want to know, you would have
to make yourself blind and deaf. Dictionaries define an
'ignoramus' as an uneducated person—but they've got it
wrong. If a shoemaker hasn't read Pushkin but stitches his
shoes well, he's not an ignoramus. He becomes one when
he pontificates on more lofty matters than footwear. Not
so long ago I was attacked by various generals over my
'Chonkin' books, and they were criticising literature as
complete ignoramuses. Many of them are graduates of two
military academies, and if they stayed within their area of
expertise, and talked about the way to command regiments
and divisions, I probably wouldn't refer to them as
ignoramuses. But what do they do? . . . Anyway, every man
and his dog has lectured literary authors—generals and
general secretaries alike. In Khrushchev's time there was
a young woman working on a kolkhoz, a heroine of Socialist
labour, called Zaglada. She lectured us as well. And so the
famous actor Gribov made the comment that 'everyone in
our country understands culture, from Khrushchev to
Zaglada, but gherkins are three rubles a kilogram at the
market.' That was expensive then. Of course the numbers
would be different now. Although in fact, the value of the
Russian ruble is holding steady. Nothing has any effect on

it, neither the war in Afghanistan, nor our own conflict in Chechnya. Our oil production is stable. Actually, different countries have different standards of economic well-being. When the NATO countries were bombing Yugoslavia, I asked my friend in Belgrade, Moma Dimic, how they would survive. 'Your whole economy's going to be destroyed,' I said. 'Rubbish,' said Moma. 'We have always got by on scarce resources, for our entire history. We make a vegetable garden in our back yard, plant some potatoes, then we dig them up, and we have food. And that gives us enough to survive. Anything more is a luxury, which you can do without.' That was my father's attitude as well. He was the ultimate ascetic—he always used to say: 'Bread and water—there's a diet for fine lads.' And he lived by that principle. He didn't eat meat, fish, milk, eggs, fruit or vegetables. So what did he eat, you ask? Bread and water—that's what. OK, from time to time he might indulge in some potatoes or kasha—but that's all. I'm no ascetic, and have sampled all the gourmet delights in my time, but in my childhood I lived through two, or more accurately one and a half, true famines, and I will always remember that when you are really hungry, the simplest food tastes better than the most sophisticated dishes. In fact the normal man or woman doesn't need all that much to be happy. The academician Boris Viktorovich Rauschenbach used to tell me that the best days of his life and career had been his time in a prison camp. He was there because of his German origins, but didn't feel hard done by, and was working on something to do with rocket construction—not for any financial reward, but because he enjoyed it. Because of that he was exempted from physical labour, and his remuneration was—prison gruel. In any other country he would have had research assistants and a staff of people working for him, and would have been paid handsomely. The outcome would then clearly have been different, but the enjoyment he got from his work probably wouldn't have been any greater. Now I'm not in favour of prison camps or famines, but it's true that a high standard of living deprives human beings of their strongest sensations, what I call our 'primal joys'. I spent the first one and a half years of my military service in Poland. Our unit was stationed in a small town, behind enclosures—which were sometimes stone walls, sometimes barbed wire fences. We didn't get any leave, and we really suffered from the lack of freedom. But occasionally, with my friend Vovka Grachev, I managed to crawl out under the barbed wire and walk around on the other side, among the bushes growing up against the fence. Never in my life have I felt such joy from a sense of freedom as I did in those bushes. In 1943 I was eleven years old, and I was living with an aunt in a small town near Samara. There was a dreadful famine, people were starving, swelling up and dying, sometimes right on the street. And perhaps I would have died too, but my father arrived. After being severely wounded and spending eight months in hospital, he was living in the country with my mother, and turned up with a sack over his shoulder, or a 'sidor', as the slang term used to be. He undid the sidor, and started taking out pieces of dripping. When I saw this I almost cried with disappointment, remembering how dripping had always made me feel sick. But I still took a bit, licked it, took a tentative bite—and . . . I have never tasted anything so delicious, before or since. Could any artichokes, crayfish or oysters ever compare with it? Can the satisfaction of a rich man buying his tenth villa ever compare with the joy of moving out of a communal flat into your own apartment? And what about reading? Now you can simply buy any book and read it. But it's hard to find the time, and why bother, what with your business, the computer, the Internet, television and the soap operas. I was eight years old when I graduated from children's picture books to real, thick books. That was in Stavropol, on a farmstead on the steppe, with snow drifts outside up to the roof. There was nothing to do, nowhere to go, during the long, long days. And if I had had television, a computer and the Internet, would I have started reading?—like Hell I would. Now on TV I see optimists arguing that children read books now as well—it's just that they start later. But reading is like playing the violin—you have to start from earliest childhood. Those children start later, and stop earlier. There is no incentive for them. During the samizdat days, what a joy it was to devour a semi-legible manuscript, that you had for just one night, risking big trouble if you were caught! There's a story about a grandmother who wanted to teach her grandson to read. They say she typed *War and Peace* out and gave it to him as a samizdat work, because even at that age he wasn't interested in ordinary books. I always used to think that nothing needed freedom more than literature. But it turns out that in conditions of complete freedom literature chokes, like a cactus plant in fertile chernozem soil. Of course freedom is the most precious gift, and even if it harms literature I'm nonetheless for freedom, but still it's a shame, there's no getting away from it. The great writers used to hold people's minds in thrall, but now that power has been transferred to TV commentators and presenters. Just as I write, there's a woman on the screen asking 'and what is your attitude to masturbation?' The other woman, looking like modesty itself, replies that she is all in favour of it, and says she masturbated while watching porn videos. In an earlier programme, some general or other had been horrified at 'what the world was coming to'. But then again, not everyone finds it so horrifying. One guy I know wrote in a newspaper that watching porn was pretty pointless, but up to the age of fourteen, why not? The other woman, giggling (she clearly did feel a little bit embarrassed after all), told us from the TV set that masturbation was best of all when you were in the shower—with a flexible hose and a strong jet of water, you reached orgasm straight away. Thank goodness for the remote—I pressed the control, the discussion of masturbation ceased, and we had the spectacle of a fireside chat with some greybeard dramatist, complaining that 'they' (who?—the American imperialists perhaps?) were corrupting him. If they were, they had already corrupted themselves good and proper. And now they had started on him. They were broadcasting all sorts of rubbish, he said, which he sat, watched and suffered through, and yet in the old days everything had been soooo good. We read good books, watched good plays and programmes, went to visit one another, and we were all so kind to one another. 'Kindness—that's what's missing these days,' he said, with a distinctly malevolent look. And I couldn't help remembering the kindly folk who played cat-and-mouse with Akhmatova, Zoshchenko, Pasternak and Galich (modesty forbids me to mention my own case). Those offices, closed sessions, open meetings, indignant letters from the workers with their kindly suggestions for dealing with the situation: expel them, exile them, or shoot them like mad dogs. Mandelstam said that poetry had never been valued so highly as in our country—because they kill you for it. Now they don't kill you any more, and it's become boring. Recently a sociologist told me that for today's youth the most prestigious profession is to be an auditor, followed by banker, manager, lawyer and dentist. Diplomats were in twenty-somethingth position, behind fashion designers, beauticians and chefs in high-class restaurants. I asked him where writers had come, and he expressed embarrassment that he hadn't read that far down the list. They say we don't have many genuinely talented writers. That's because the writer's gift is unique. Good writers are far rarer than good bankers or dentists or even heart surgeons. The writer's job is one of the hardest. And what does a good writer usually get for his labours? It's not a matter of money alone, but that is part of the problem. I have been involved in literature for forty years, and have always worked hard and conscientiously. I have been fortunate enough to attract some attention. My books are still being printed in large numbers, and sometimes I get a decent return. But then there are years when I earn nothing at all. Many people like my work, they write me letters and tell me about it, but I have also had more insulting comments than any incompetent fitter, carpenter or concierge would ever have to deal with. Whatever they call me: a writer, a renegade, a pig who bites the hand that feeds it or a pug dog barking at an elephant, or a cockroach—thank you, kind people, you haven't praised me, and you're quite right. That's what Viktor Nikolaevich Ilyin—KGB general and secretary of the Writers' Union—once told me, quoting some luminary of Marxist thought. Viktor Nikolaevich himself was my enemy, come to that. He never praised me, but sometimes, thumping the corner of his desk, he used to ask me in a whisper (wary of the hidden microphones he assumed were there): 'Do you really believe anyone's ever going to publish your "Chonkin" novel?' I replied 'It's not a matter of believing it—I know it'll be published!' 'Conceited, aren't you?' he mocked. 'You're the conceited one,' I told him. 'You think you're in control of this period of history. But in fact you're just passing through, and there's one thing you can't understand—down through the ages, in every nation, banned books have always outlived the people who ban them.' Viktor Nikolaevich lived to see me proved right. I'm told he was in the office of *Yunost* magazine, and when he heard 'Chonkin' was going to be published in the next issue he threw up his hands in astonishment and sat there for a long time, scratching his head. The poor man—to think it had come to this! Never mind, he died not long afterwards—run over by a truck in mysterious circumstances. People ask me what has helped me to survive everything I have had to live through. And that's my answer: my awareness that bans and prohibitions were only temporary, and that there could only be relative value in benefits gained by forsaking those things I regarded as being of absolute value. Until now I've never said much about myself in public, and have ignored all the slanderous accusations levelled against me—that I ridicule the sufferings of the people and look down on everyone as fools—the fools are the people who talk like that, and it's true, I do look down on and ridicule them. But these days I do get angry sometimes, and here's what I'd like to say to these fine folk—whatever sort of man I was, I'm not like you, kind people, in that I never lied, stole, eavesdropped, crawled to the authorities, or made a career out of other people's suffering, and in the hard times, those very hard times when those kindly folk held sway in the departments and paid social calls on one another, I told the truth with a smile—who to?—tsars?—no, not to the tsars, but to whatever bastard I was dealing with. I may well put these words in the mouth of one of the characters in my new book that I haven't found a title for yet. Yesterday I had a phone call from one of our prestigious literary periodicals, asking me when it would be finished. I said, soon. They told me that was what I said last year. I replied that I had thought it would be soon—it didn't turn out that way, but this time it really would be soon. It'll be there—soon. Very soon. Time passes quickly, much faster than we used to think. When I was young I couldn't imagine living to see what's happening now. And look at me now—once I used to be younger than all my friends, and now I'm just about the oldest. Arnold McMillin is getting ready to celebrate a landmark birthday which for me is far in the past. Someone's putting out a periodical issue dedicated to him—I should submit something dedicated to Arnold. And who knows, maybe I will. A stream of consciousness piece—a mixture of thoughts on this and that. But it's night at the moment, the TV is on, it's that 'Smart Walker' programme, an erotic comedy, a thriller, more besides, and . . . maybe that's enough for now. How does that poem by David Samoilov go? 'Off to bed, sleepy and fully informed, the shadow on the tube flickers and dies'—that can't be right. But who cares? The something or other on the tube flickers and dies, and so does my consciousness. Or was it 'flickers into life'? Ah, got it—the slit on the tube flickers and dies.

Translated from the Russian by John Jamieson

Hipólito G. Navarro

Hipólito G. Navarro was born in 1961 in Huelva in the south of Spain, although he has lived in Seville since 1979. I le trained as a biologist but never worked in that field, and thus describes himself as a 'biologus interruptus'. His first collection of short stories was published in 1990 and was followed at regular intervals by further collections. *Los últimos percances* (The Latest Mishaps), which was awarded the prestigious Mario Vargas Llosa Prize for Best Collection of Short Stories in Spain in 2005, brings together most of his published short stories and some which have not previously appeared in print. The selection panel praised Navarro's non-conformist approach to literature, which combines multiple registers of language, humour and innovative uses of narrative techniques.

Base Times Height Divided By Two

1

Of course, from this vantage point, with an iced black coffee, sitting in the shade of the lime tree on the avenue, seeing the green of the two acacia trees next to the porch, if I were a painter right now I'd be picking up my palette and brushes, painting the relaxed peace of the cool mountain siesta, with this breeze weaving around my crossed legs where I sit opposite him, as he redrafts a letter to far-off friends; obviously, that's what I'd do if I were a painter.

But in the meantime, until this interest in oils and pigments becomes something more than a mere stain on a hypothetical painter's smock, I'll try wide-eyed to absorb the greens and blues of the acacias against the holiday sky. Enfolded in this peace—I hear the trickle of the fountain close by—that the afternoon will bring, hinting at the milder August to come, in my head, as usual, I'll be forced to draw in the white line of the porch roof from which two dizzied boys stare down at the lines of ants below, attracted by the sunflower seed husks flicked onto the ground by bored couples.

Those two boys on the porch could easily be my brother and me in the distant past of this village, and me, the one writing this because painting is beyond me, sitting next to him, the one who is still redrafting in his lovingly crafted script a letter to friends who become present as he writes, he and I, now, we could easily be two foreigners like the ones who travel to tourist destinations to write letters and contemplate through foreign eyes children playing in piles of sand around porches. But we're not foreigners. Ah, those two kids on the porch, risking life and limb right up there as high as they can get. Ah, the holidays, providing a glimpse of those two kids up there and taking my memory back twenty-five or thirty years to see myself again, cavorting in the sand, playing those poor kids' games with dirt and sticks, such happiness crouched down in readiness for the onslaught of tears; it'd be better to just forget it all.

Right, and then I'm painting on my retina the columns that separate the porch railings, rust splashed down like paint by the rain, and seen from here, from this vantage point without brushes, the height of the porch roof is a huge, skull-cracking multiple of the height of those little kids who could be me and my brother, my brother and me, making the most of the cheap entertainment of the sand pile, beggars can't be choosers, while the neighbours rev up their Scalextric and build Babylons with their Meccano sets, much to the envy of us dirt-diggers.

Ah, the holidays, another year on this avenue in our childhood village, escaping from the furnace of the city to this place tainted by the past, sitting down again—he and I—at this marble-topped table under the lime tree with the blackest of black coffees, him writing his friendly little writing to friends who seem almost present right here in these words that slither across the page like curly snails. If I were a painter, from where I sit, looking at the porch the way I am doing, and the two rather prissy-looking kids on the sand heap, I would paint what I see and as well as the railings I should put in an extra wall to keep the kids' games away from the yawning abyss, maybe I'd paint a lawn below as well, a soft cushion in case of predictable accidents, instead of the drunken broken bottles left by bored couples under the acacias at night, couples sitting on the porch where—who'd have believed it—you can make out the nightingales' April song.

But of course, how can anyone stop it happening, how can anyone from this privileged position of the tourist call out in English or Norwegian when the boy—one of the pair, it doesn't matter which—when the boy has scrambled up to the highest part of the porch roof, and the other boy—one of the pair, it doesn't matter which—the other one tries to restrain his ill-timed Icarian desire to fly, how can anyone intercept the fall of the boy who ends up way down there, broken, amidst the shards of glass, interrupting his poor kids' games in the dirt to become more closely involved with the earth in the cemetery? Ay! Sitting here, how could anyone not remember, from this privileged position I can calculate the height that swallowed up my twin brother after a gentle little push that did away, accidentally in the saddened eyes of a whole village, with a child they considered a little angel but who for me meant nothing but the halving of the family budget, the leech-like reason that I got nothing but huge piles of sand pissed on by dogs instead of Monopoly sets and skates?

Ah, those bitter holidays that, on summer afternoons like these, not only offer the privileged drowsy shade of the lime trees, but also point at me from the branches of the acacias with accusing fingers that most likely saw my sinister intent towards the toys that weren't there, that I couldn't even write a letter to, while my neighbours were so happy with the results of their letters to the Three Wise Men, who generously delivered the goods on the morning of the Epiphany. Damn those holiday memories! From then on I was able to build up piles upon piles of presents, including very quickly the whitest notebooks to write grisly stories in; since his brother passed away, this boy can't seem to do anything but write unhappy stories, that tortured imagination of his, sometimes there are unfathomable depths in his eyes, where do these torments come from? Even in that essay about a cow set by the teacher, instead of some nice grass and milk and baby bulls he puts in vets probing for tumours, and cowboys sticking their big, sweaty, hairy hands into the cow's enormous vagina to pull out dead calves, how horrible! Really horrible!

Ah, the holidays, the holidays, forcing me back like a sleepwalker to that table to watch over the murderous memory of those toys. We wouldn't have needed that many of them, because at the end of the day, those yearnings were satisfied by a few pens and paper to write violent, dirty stories, grotesque accessories after the fact; we wouldn't have needed so many suitcases for that horrible trip, because my brother didn't need the toys that I didn't need either in the end; his thing was painting, he would've been a painter, and an eleven-year-old artist isn't that expensive to supply: a small box of crayons and a silly little box of watercolours, my little brother, he didn't even need paper, just as happy with a glass of water free from the fountain and a handful of white stones free from the quarry to embellish in a myriad of colours with any old cheap brush. Such a pity! There's still a basket of painted stones on the landing of my mother's stairs at home, a bright memory of an angel felled by a greedy shove.

2

Still writing that letter to your friends? I asked him, wiping my oily hands on the mucky hem of my smock, my eyes all the while measuring with surprise the skull-cracking height of the porch railings, and he, little bastard, replying, looking at me over the top of the canvas, draining his coffee, that it wasn't a letter but rather a story, one of those short stories like your brother probably used to write before his fatal fall. Of course, always reminding me of that tragedy, horrible holidays that bring me back to this spot under the lime tree where, with my very expensive beaver hair brushes, I paint that bitch of a vertical drop heightened by my toys, and to top it off seeing two kids on the porch who could be—why not?—in the leafy distant past of the acacia shadows, me and my brother, my brother and me, the two of us, inventing poor kids' games on a pile of dirt left over from building work done for the rich parents of kids with toy cars and dolls that do everything, for fuck's sake, from talking and whistling to shutting their eyes and even pissing.

More bloody holidays, coming back for another summer with my box of paint tubes and the easel and the unfinished canvas from those other times when I disguised the porch railings of my criminal solution, outlining in blood red a wall to make me rethink the shove and possibly avoid that camouflaged accident, those reptilian crocodile tears when my brother was already broken, down there amongst the shattered glass. What an excessive response to the restricted family budget, what a wicked way of ending the constant dividing that lurked at the heart of my hunger for toys!

Ah the holidays, the horrible holidays in this childhood village. If only I could write halfway decently—yeah, that's it, if only—I'd try to form the letters to spell out the conspiratorial silences of those two acacia trees by the porch, to find the adjectives I need to describe unflinchingly the shocking height of the wall, to sum up in an accurate sentence the secret hypocrisy of that simple game, those two kids on the porch with the sand and the sticks, only a few inches from the edge of the abyss. I'd write about that, if I were a writer of course, instead of standing here producing this verb-less explosion of colour on canvas.

Yeah, that's it, while he's sitting there writing, or so he says, a story like the ones my brother used to write, a Mozart of the pencil at eleven shattered on the rocks of my longed-for toys. Ill will, gulped like rotten milk in anxious swallows from the twin breast that I clutched, at the same time clutching the other breast too, and him, my twin brother, in the cradle, not yet aware of the milk that would be wasted because of my hunger for toys.

The fucking holidays, so many summers returning to the shade of the lime tree, never ever being able to finish that gradually stiffening canvas, the tubes of colours splitting open under the accusing gaze of the acacia fingers that sensed my plans to monopolise the whole of the toy budget, plans that needn't have been that radical in the end, because since then my thing has been collecting boards and pots of colour to draw burning landscapes, portraits of monsters. Since his brother passed away, this kid can't seem to paint anything but horror scenes, that tortured imagination of his, sometimes you can see hell and purgatory in his eyes, where does such torment come from?— even in that picture of mountains set by the teacher he leaves out the flowers and the shepherds and the little lambs and instead he plants crosses where witches are being burnt, seemingly laughing while snakes and pens pour out of their gaping mouths, how awful! Yes, how appalling his drawings are!

Ah, the dreadful holidays, trying to finish a canvas with the sticky complicity of the oil paints winking colours at me; oh, the endless sketching of this anguish that resists being painted, all this so that he, sitting there writing a story like the ones my absent brother used to write, can see how useless my brushes are, and he smiles on yet another afternoon and repeats that joke, funny but sick, of why don't you paint that thing about base times height divided by two that you do so well, damn him.

Ah the holidays, these damned holidays, there in front of the porch where the kids are, him here at my side eyeing me suspiciously, and me, the one splashing paint about because writing is something that is beyond me, downing iced black coffee under the lime tree, remembering that hunger for toys. I wouldn't actually have needed so many, in the end the yearning was to be satisfied with a handful of marker pens and crayons and the shocking violence of a few paintings, dirty accessories after the fact, too much luggage for such a short trip, because basically my brother cared as little about toys as I did, his thing was writing, and a writer barely eleven years old is hardly expensive: a flimsy folder with some paper and a couple of pencils to be chewed in the excitement of writing stories. Such a pity! His slender little volume of handwritten stories, lovingly bound in leather, is still on the shelf in my mother's living room, a memorial to an angel felled by excessive ambition.

3

Obviously, from this vantage point, with our iced black coffees, sitting under the lime tree on the avenue—the spouts of the fountain splashing water so close and resonant—my brother and I, seeing as we do the green of the two acacias next to the porch, can't really do anything except in his case paint a canvas with the colours and lights of the height, and in mine write a parallel story about the yawning abyss strewn with broken glass. Because, of course, contemplating the games of the two kids in a pile of sand only a few inches from eternity, it's perfectly logical that we spontaneously exchange knowing and remembering glances, unearthed from twenty-five or thirty years before, when my brother and me, me and my brother, innocently played poor kids' games in the dirt, each imagining a mistaken happiness of expensive toys that would be more likely if one of the two were to disappear, but thanks to that strange telepathy between twins, when I was about to shove him and he was about to shove me, our wicked intentions and the non-existent toys, so alike in each of our minds, were transformed into a hug, as we looked out from the very brink of death at what would surely have been a half life, mutilated by the loss of our inseparable other. And now, of course, from this vantage point, we, the we of twenty-five or thirty years later, whole and in one piece, together, fortunately, one of us painting—it doesn't matter which—the other with the writing paper—it doesn't matter who—in our own similar and different ways we build the wall needed to raise the railings so that those kids rolling round in the dirt today can finish their games without predictable accidents and the porch roof can carry on untainted by tragedy under the acacias where, in the summer evenings pierced by the crickets' singing, couples sometimes get bored and where in another season, who would've thought it, the nightingales' songs stitch together the Aprils and the Mays.

Translated from the Spanish by Nicola Gilmour

Åke Smedberg

Åke Smedberg was born in Hjässberget in 1948 and now lives near Uppsala. His first book was a volume of poetry, *Inpå benen*, published in 1976. He has won a number of literary prizes, including Aftonbladet's Literature Prize and the Sven Delblanc Prize. He is also known as a crime writer.

Smedberg often writes about people with strong emotions that they cannot express. The stories here are taken from *Hässja: berättelser från en trakt* (Albert Bonniers Förlag, 2000), which won the Ivar Lo Prize in 2001.

Six Stories

Smallholding

Hov 3:11. That's the land title. A smallholding. Four and a half hectares of fields, sixteen hectares of forest.

The forest lies to the south, seen from the farm, climbing up Hjässberget's northern slope. Mostly spruce, of course. A single stand of pine, tall and straight. In the forest plot there is also a sheer cliff face, 'Gushing' it is called, on account of the water that constantly trickles down here. In winter fantastic ice shapes form under the overhanging cliffs.

Higher up there's a cold spring. A trinity spring: one that flows north, from three tributaries. In the fifties Erland and Inga-Britt draw water from here down to the house. Hand dig the whole distance, down to a depth that is free of frost. It gets difficult on the actual mountain slope, they have to break up the earth as far down as possible, covering it over with brushwood. Untold anthills are used for insulation. Still it can happen that the water freezes in wintertime, especially if the snow cover is thin. Turning the taps off completely amounts to a mortal sin. The water should always run. On sparkling cold winter nights when the thermometer creeps under thirty, Erland wanders restlessly to and fro around the house, testing the taps, trying to find the ideal position. A thin, even stream; not too little, not too much—a steady movement of water that keeps the ice at bay and yet doesn't run the spring dry.

The marvellous spring.

The water from here has special, miraculous qualities, we're always being told that. We drink, testing. Yes, maybe there is something then . . . It's certainly cold in any case . . .

So much for the forest.

And the fields? To the north—towards the stream that cuts a half circle around the property—they consist of Storlägdan and Lillnäset. To the south are Flodikslägdan and Myrlägdan. And the pasture too. The paddock next to the main road, and Kalvhagen, bordering on the stream to the west. All in all scarcely five hectares. Seven football fields.

The farmhouse and farm buildings are on the raised ridge that divides the cultivated land in half. Originally it was a summer grazing pasture. Grandfather Emil and grandmother Anna bought it and moved here some time around 1910, and for a long time they lived in the old summer grazing cottage. It wasn't until the mid thirties that the new house was built.

Farm property Hov 3:11. Hjässberget village. If you can call it a village now. A clearing in the forest. Some farms you barely have time to notice before you've gone past. A few kilometres from town. In the wrong direction, right between the big valleys. In the forest. The roads leading here a constant—and poor—joke. From the fifties to the nineties. Not a place for day trips. Those who come here have a reason. If they haven't just got lost.

The new house

In 1937 they build the new farmhouse. A two storey house in typical thirties style: mansard roof, weatherboards, Falun red with white corners and window frames. Two rooms and a kitchen downstairs, one room and alcove upstairs, plus cold attic and a number of box rooms.

It is the children who do the building. At evenings and weekends, when they can get away. Most have their own families now.

Around ten years later, in a picture from the latter half of the forties, they are all gathered in front of the new house. Eight sons and three daughters. Fredrik, Bengt, Ture, Henry, Gösta, Ivar, Bertil, Erland, Svea, Margit, Rut. Thirteen people in all, with grandfather Emil and grandmother Anna. Not exactly a lucky number. But numerology doesn't have much significance here, one way or the other. They will not be unluckier than others. Probably not luckier either, for that matter.

The men in suits, the women in dresses or smart costumes. The older sons authoritative, substantive, with immaculately knotted ties and an almost easy elegance of bearing. They could be taken for businessmen, relatively successful. Merging without much difficulty in fact into a boardroom photo of some big company. These are no farm yokels in their finery turning towards the camera. If anything betrays them it is their hands: the broad, stiff-thumbed hands of craftsmen and manual labourers, unused to unemployment, resting rather heavily on a knee or half sticking out of a jacket pocket.

In age and appearance they are a varied tribe. Nearly twenty years between the oldest and youngest. Some of the sons fair, hair already thinning, while others clearly show their Walloon heritage: jet black, unruly mops of hair and noticeably darker pigmentation.

Of the three daughters, it is the youngest who differs almost defiantly from the rest. Costume jacket with wide sleeves and padded shoulders. A necklace around the slender neck. The long hair artistically put up. A pale face, with classically pure features, almost luminously beautiful. The slightly turned down corners of her mouth give her appearance a touch of melancholy. A tragic beauty, an Anna Karenina, in the middle of central Norrland smallholding reality.

Grandfather Emil and grandmother Anna sit right in front, with their tribe of children around them. Surrounded by this abundance of sons and daughters, Emil is already marked by illness. It is cancer that is eating him from within, like a digger wasp. He will be gone within the year. His body shrivelled up where he sits, squeezing a silver-mounted walking stick with his broad hands. You can still see that he has been a tall man. At his full height probably quite as tall as the tallest of the sons. Hair still black, in spite of his being seventy years old.

Grandmother Anna, on the other hand, is already a picture of old age. Thin, stooped, white-haired, with her small hands quietly clasped in her lap. She will live a good twenty-five years more, without really changing. In fact, she will rather seem younger, decade by decade, more alert and brighter, until finally almost translucent. And always a mystery. About herself she says little or nothing. On her husband's side there is sweeping, almost ungovernable talk; with her, silence. As if she thinks there's been enough talk, more than enough.

The two eldest children sit on either side of their parents. Next to Anna is Svea. Strong, dark, radiating a kind of stern motherliness. Straight-backed, black hair only lightly permed. In spite of the smile on her lips there is something both reserved and masterful about her, an obvious authority. If anyone could be regarded as head of this company, it is quite clearly her.

Erland sits next to grandfather Emil. He is in his forties now. A sensitive face, almost weak. In fact, there is something weak, tentative about his whole bearing, in spite of the broad shoulders, tall body. He seems to be bent over a little towards Emil, his chest brushing against his father's shoulder, as if seeking support there. It is he who will take over the place, more or less against his will. He is a builder, a carpenter, with his own house down towards Siljehållet, but alone with an almost teenage daughter since his first wife died. Here he has already met Inga-Britt, he will soon be married again, with a new family on the way.

He is perhaps not best suited to be a farmer, but, as already mentioned, he is the eldest son, the one on whom the responsibility falls, whether he wants it or not.

This you can see in the picture. With a little background knowledge of those depicted you can read something of their personalities and lives in their facial expressions and poses, allow them to appear as individuals.

But in reality of course the picture says nothing of all this. Nothing about their thoughts, dreams, characters, their future or their past. All it says is that here they are right now, frozen in time, on that early summer's day (you can tell the time exactly from the young leaves on the birch that is just visible at the edge of the picture), in front of the house they built for their parents.

They could be any smallholding family. There is nothing special about them. No more so than anyone else. Ordinary people. As ordinary as everyone. And as mysterious.

The horse

The horse is the first animal. It is forged from the wind by some early deity, who later sinks in among the shadows, forgotten, erased, until what finally remains of him is merely a moment's silence. A scarcely noticeable empty space or a hesitation in the introduction to some myths in a long dead language.

But the horse remains. Enters the service of new gods, who will also be forgotten, wither away and vanish, drifting away like dust over the grassy sea of the steppes.

It rises up out of rivers and lakes, foaming white and green-eyed. Or grazes in jet black herds on the grasslands near some entrance to the underworld. Draws the sun's burning chariot across the vaulted sky. Is ridden by a bloodthirsty, one-eyed old man through the stunted forests of the north.

But always with something shying away, unapproachable in its misty gaze. There's a remoteness there, that tells of it not really belonging to anyone, neither gods nor humans. Deep down inside it is still wind . . .

Erland has grown up with horses, imbued with them so to speak. When he talks about horses he undergoes a gradual change. Perhaps not directly into a horse, but—in fact—something horse-like certainly surfaces. He becomes rather dedicated and at the same time completely relaxed, unselfconscious, like the play of muscles in a freely running horse. His face with its large, crooked nose seems to grow longer, more elongated. His laugh snorting, neighing.

He leans back, eyes screwed up, gazing into the distance; lets them take shape, come walking, trotting, whinnying . . .

In practical terms, in his way of relating to and handling horses, there is something intuitive, self-evident. Seldom any open emotion, one way or the other. Rather a kind of distance, something of an exchange of views between equals. When he has adjusted the harness and bridle he can be standing motionless for a while beside the horse and you get a feeling of a wordless debate going on, where they are both mutually examining and assessing each other, discussing what will be done, what is desirable and what is possible, and, after arguing the toss, meeting half way.

Afterwards they return to their respective worlds. The horse to its horse world, the man to his smallholding world.

He probably doesn't give much thought to this ability, seeing it as something natural, acquired through experience. Yet a significant part of his life will pass without horses. From his twenties he works more or less permanently as a builder, raises a family, builds a house of his own down towards Siljedalen, not far from town. Certainly he works off and on in the forest in winter, but he is approaching forty before he finally returns to the smallholding and the horse, taking over the place up at Hjässberget.

He never really becomes a farmer. There's an ambivalence there, over being forced to return to something he already thinks he has left. An indifference, as if none of it really concerns him.

The horses are another matter. There is never any doubt or uncertainty—quite the opposite. It is a landscape where he moves with a kind of natural, sovereign authority. As when he steps in between the flailing front hooves of a high-spirited young horse, grips it with a hand over its nostrils and pulls it firmly back down again.

He doesn't buy a tractor until well into the sixties—a second-hand Ferguson. And it's never more than an extra. A means of transport for less skilled tasks. For Erland the horse is still the primary focus, the hub his world revolves around. Of course he realises that it belongs to the past, but that doesn't bother him. Probably he has already begun to see himself from the same perspective.

There is an application from the beginning of the seventies for an improvement loan for property Hov 3:11. In the column for other assets he has noted in his loosely elegant handwriting: One horse. Nothing else. No chattels, savings, cash, etc.

It could be seen as a kind of wry sarcasm. But probably he had no such thought. It is simply a statement. He has declared what is important. A horse. Nothing more need be said.

When he dies—a little over ten years later—it is in keeping too that he is on his way out to the stable.

It is Whitsun week, early morning. Everything suddenly stands still; the world fractures, ceases to exist. He drops down dead in the grass, struck by a massive heart attack. To lie full length on his back, a few metres from the stable doors.

There is no one nearby. Except the horse, moving restlessly inside the stable building. Scents his smell, kicks against the walls, snorts, screams, from thirst and longing.

Cows

Cows. We never have more than three or four, sometimes just two. Some heifers, some calves.

In an early, almost transparent memory they still go to the forest. Within earshot, on the steep slope up towards Hjässberget. They come jogging, heavy-uddered, through the filtering evening light, on their way home. Swarms of gnats like smoke around their bodies, where angular and plump blend together in a bewildering mix. The bony, almost sharp-edged hindquarters, the drum-tight distended stomachs, striking heavy udders.

There is a busybody air about them as they come trotting along, mooing agitatedly, as if they have been exposed to some injustice and are now on their way to hold the guilty to account. A troop of aunts, striding energetically along in the gravel.

But the most beautiful thing is their eyes. Veiled. Velvety soft. Far-seeing, but inward-looking, towards an inner, constantly receding horizon. The mysterious emptiness in their gaze. No dreams, nothing. Just this pure, calm emptiness. Like the surface of water, where nothing stirs.

Svana. Krusa. Lisskulla. The names linger on, a succession of names you can't get free of. Others come after them, but they are never really replaced. When a cow dies, goes for slaughter, a noticeable silence arises, an empty space.

The horse is work and luxury in one. But the cow is life. From her body flows life. Everything about her is life. Calves, milk, manure, meat . . .

The grief for a cow is unobtrusive, quiet, but long lasting. Old tethers are left hanging unused for years. 'No, leave it hanging. It's Svana's. It wouldn't do anyway. She was so strong across the shoulders. There aren't many like her . . .'

And days, weeks beforehand they seem to sense the arrival of the butcher's car. Stay out in the pasture, remain stubbornly standing. Withdraw from attempts to touch them, the awkward pats on neck and back. As if they are preparing themselves, steeling themselves.

To begin with it is Inga-Britt who looks after the barn. From the sixties, when she begins working nights at the hospital, Erland increasingly takes over. Morning milking before he goes off to the forest or a construction job, spring and autumn. Does the evening milking too when he comes home at dusk.

Hand milking, this is. He sits with his forehead resting against the cow's side, squeezing the milk from the teats with rhythmical, caressing hand movements. Mutters, swears, when any of the animals steps away or gives a kick. 'Now now! Stand still for God's sake!' But the cows don't take much notice of his cursing and swearing. Just turn their big heads, give him an almost mischievous look from their dark eyes, a coquettish little swish of their tails.

Towards the end of the sixties the last cow disappears, and with it also the real farming. It means later mornings, at last. But something else is changed too. Something deeper, more fundamental. Erland has perhaps always been a half-hearted farmer, but the land has still in some way made him timeless, ageless. The years have not left their mark on him, not caught up with him. Now he suddenly notices how they are snapping at his heels. Time is getting on.

He talks about a dream, where a white cow stands above him, licking him on the face. He is lying in the grass, his hat over his eyes. Like at haymaking, when they sank down to rest for a while at midday. Then he feels that rough, warm tongue on his face and jumps up. No, of course he can't get up. As always in dreams it's hard to move, but he must have got rid of the hat, because he can see the cow above him.

And she continues licking him. Calmly, methodically, as if he were a calf that should be licked clean. Then she is gone and finally he can get up. When he catches sight of her again she is already far away, crossing the stream. She goes in and comes out on the other side.

And now suddenly she is black and larger than any cow he has seen. And yet she moves softly, cat-like. He feels the hairs rising on the back of his neck, in a terror he can't explain, as he sees the huge black cow somehow gliding forward through the scrub on the other side of the stream . . .

Inga-Britt looks at him rather concerned. He laughs, shakes his head, waves it all away . . . It's just a dream, dreams don't mean anything, it's just the brain playing.

But it's obvious that he doesn't really believe it. That he knows the dream meant something for him. That the black cow has come, that she is there somewhere nearby.

Wind church, grass church

Erland on the chair out under the birches. Hair thin and white. It is the first—and only—time I cut it for him.

'Just trim it a little,' he says.

The beginning of the eighties. He is seventy-three. The white wisps drift like thistledown in the wind. He smiles, shaking his head slightly.

'There's not much for the birds to build nests with . . .'

Face tanned, burnt brown. But in the gap under his shirt collar his skin shines blue-white as skim milk, defenceless somehow. And the sparse hair under my hands. Soft, like a child's. We shall never see each other again, never touch each other. Naturally we don't know that. We suspect it perhaps, but it's not something we talk about. We just chat. The words travel lightly, floating on the wind. In the distance the forest glistens in the sun.

'Up there, on Skvalbranten, we were driving late one autumn, Fredrik and I . . .'

He nods up towards Hjässberget's steep side.

'We'd have been about nine or ten, I suppose. There was a load of wood that had to be brought home. We didn't have frost nails and it was frozen and icy. The horse slid off the road, rolled full length down into the bushes on the side. But we got him up, drove home and put on frost nails. Then he just climbed up as if he was going upstairs! It was probably the first time we were out in the forest on our own. Father was out felling and we were the eldest, Fredrik and I. We were like the men of the house . . .'

Distant memories that he fishes up, examines with amusement, releases into the wind. An inward-looking smile on his long, angular face. I stand leaning over him, squeezing unpractised scissors that keep catching in the soft hair. Think of the times when I sat here myself, sobbing when the scissors tore out tufts of hair, felt his broad hands straighten up my head, heard him grunt impatiently, 'Sit still, so I don't cut your ears off!'

He is gentler now, milder. And at the same time more distant. He is moving away, through a vast space of wind and grass. Further and further away.

Sled tracks

Up towards Skarpåsen, in mid February. Logging, where Erland has taken on both cutting and driving.

I am fourteen. Home from school for some reason. Winter holidays perhaps. Or I may have just stayed home anyway, it's not unusual.

There isn't much left to do. What remains is mostly the

clearing up. A few pieces of pulpwood that have been lying in the snow and need to go out to the main forest road. Some marked timber to be felled.

I gather it up and help load. Am allowed to take the chainsaw and trim a section where Erland has felled. Mostly for something to do, to pass the time. All the while he stands off to one side behind me, supervising, as if he doesn't really dare leave me. And he soon takes over, tearing off the branches with sweeping, practised movements.

He doesn't instruct, gives neither criticism nor praise. And why should he? He lets me try my hand, but as a momentary diversion, a game. He knows of course that this is not something I will devote my life to. I'll never get up at five in the morning to get myself off to the forest, with the darkness and cold like a wall outside. Nor does he wish it: why should you wear yourself out in the forest, if you can avoid it?

There's low cloud, grey and cold, down to fifteen below all day. As long as you're moving it's all right, but when we take a break and sit down, the cold quickly creeps into our bodies, the skin on our faces stiffens, the tears start stinging. It's best to get up again, as soon as possible, continue walking around.

Getting on for three we turn for home. It gets dark quickly. And the cold is somehow paralysing, a crunching bite to the neck. Erland sits motionless in the centre of the logging sled. I walk or jog along behind, trying to keep warm. All around is the forest, dark and chill. It feels oppressive, suffocating, like being stuck fast in a rat trap of cold and dark.

Down towards Sandmoarna you can glimpse the light from the town, a distant, pale dome on the horizon. But not down there either—in the self-important little town with its sluggish river and its boastful stone houses—is there any real freedom.

I have to leave, get away from here!

Erland's hunched back in the deepening dusk. He doesn't seem to feel the cold, just shakes himself now and then. If you just keep reasonably calm, don't rush around using up energy unnecessarily, then you won't freeze, he usually instructs. When you're working you should move about, but not unnecessarily then either, just as much as it takes.

Almost everything he talks about has to do with work. Everyday things, without making any particular points. Physical labour. On the farm, on building sites, in the forest. Sheer hard work. Yet the stories can gleam with life, and a peculiar delight. As when he almost sensually recalls some really awful felling, in a bottomless bog, where the forest grew downwards rather than upwards, a winter so freezing that a stay in Siberia would seem a real package holiday . . . Work and life have always been one and the same to him.

But right now he is silent, lost in thought, remote. As if there is no longer anything to say, either about work or anything else. It serves no purpose, has no meaning. What he knows, what he understands, no one will make use of. It belongs to the past, is set in a bygone landscape.

The horse walking on in the dark, the sled moving in the icy runner tracks. Erland's back up there. There is a boundary between us, a distance that is steadily growing. That is how it is. That is how it will be, I realise. Him there, enclosed in himself. Myself here, going my way.

Translated from the Swedish by Pleasance Purser

Amélie Plume

Amélie Plume was born in La Chaux-de-Fonds and studied literature, history and ethnology at the University of Neuchâtel. She published her first book in 1981 and has since also written for the theatre and radio. She has won a number of prizes: the Schiller Prize in 1988 for the whole of her work, the Pittard de l'Andelyn Prize in 1993, and the Fondation Radio Bâle Prize in 1997. *Oui Émile pour la Vie* was originally published by Editions Zoé in 1984 and has been reprinted several times since, most recently in 2006.

Émile For Ever . . . Amen

Prologue

'I could just eat you Up
that cute little face of yours
and down There too'
'Who's stopping you?'

> The bliss of
> his arms around me
> of his eyes In mine
> and his mouth
> on Mine
>
> together

Always For ever
together
As long as we live
TILL DEATH US DO PART
amen

A few years Later
ALSO
in the early morning

Him
spruce and chic
Grey suit pink shirt fresh shaven in a perfumed cloud of
       Aftershave
      attaché case in hand
            the young Go-getter
            on the ladder of success
'Bye Darling Have a good day'

      Her
      Grubby Dressing gown
      baby on her shoulder Dribbling
            I told you
            it's not Worth washing this Dressing
            gown
A second baby clinging on her skirts

'Good Shitty day!'

        *   *   *

I met him
I met Him . . . Hmm
      I don't exactly remember WHERE

I met him the First time
We used to go to the same school
I knew his name But *he* was A Senior
and I wasn't looking his way
Anyway *I* was in love with someone else

One day
We danced together
He and I
ALMOST by chance

He had beautiful brown eyes
so Gentle When he looked at me

          *   *   *

Love It's easy
up to this point it's Always beautiful you'll tell Me
The beginning's Always beautiful
The dawn
Those Very first instants
      The same that Later bring nostalgia
      into our homes
      No It's not like It Was before

always Wonderful The First moments
always Exciting
      No It's not like It Was before
Always thrilling

We could spend HOURS writing about the two lovebirds
we could write Pages about them
      The two of them dancing Closer and tighter
      The first little kiss on the Ear one More on

the neck
And then a Third and then Another
ET CETERA

The two of them talking together Talking
about themselves
Gazing at each other
gazing and GAZING and TALKING about
themselves
Never tiring of talking And taking each Other
in

Then HIM
springing into Action
fired with Sudden determination
BUT with trembling hand
undoing Her bra
for the very first time

and that other hand moving Up
her leg and then
slipping Above the knee
and . . . oh oh heavens
No It's not like It Was before

and while we're talking of hands
two Others two Smaller ones
tugging to open the buckle of
a heavy belt
and then
impatient buttocks
wriggling themselves free
of constricting pants
Always exciting always Thrilling

those first moments
I wonder would it still be Interesting
Even with the Dumbest guy
The First time?

How True it is
the First time we look good
There's no bad breath
no yawning
no flu No sniffly nose
What's more
we listen
don't criticise And if his Clothes Are ugly
we love him Even more
the first time
          it doesn't last
          of course
          that's Just how it is
          the first time
          It's how we are

If only we could keep that emotion our whole lives long
keep the excitement of the early days
the impatience
YES Keep that impatience our WHOLE life long
the Ultimate dream
the beautiful Impossible dream
          But when I think of it
          it can't be too easy
          to stay Impatient a Whole life long

          I wish you would kiss me
          for HOURS on end
          Granted Voilà

I'd like to sleep ALL night with you
Voilà Granted

I'd like to sleep EVERY night with you
Voilà . . .

I'd like us to have the same bedroom
. . . Granted

I wish
Voilà

I wish
I wish
I wish

granted
granted
granted

Hey ENOUGH now
Puh LEEAASE

*   *   *

Mother was white and Blue
like the Virgin Mary
She was gentle and loved her three children
more than anything else in the whole world
She was a Mary too
although for us
her three little dwarfs
her darlings She was always MUMMY

It Wasn't Joseph that Mary married
        My father would have ENTHRONED himself
        for all to see
        atop the donkey Rather than leading it humbly
        walking alongside
        There was nothing of a Joseph in Him
        He was more like a thundering King Ubu
        a juicy steak tartar bright Red
        GENEROUSLY seasoned

       *   *   *

WITH King Ubu and the Virgin Mary
I was a happy child
And though the two appeared
in our family tableau by Turns
rather than figuring TOGETHER
It didn't affect My own little world

But it's now . . . Even today
that I find it difficult
        Me who am
        part MY mother And part my father
        blue-White AND Peppery red
to reconcile
the Steak tartar AND the Madonna
WITHIN me
        How can you
        be a Woman gentle and kind
        a loving mother
        without having to Hold your tongue
        being MEEK
        Waiting on the edge
        being sad

Without being like her?

Be a woman
and be Like Him?
A woman like Him
Does that even exist?

What is there then?
WHAT?
And WHAT kind of a man could I love?

A King Ubu
like him?
No not a chance
for then I'd become Like her

A Joseph
content to lead the donkey
IN SILENCE?
Then wouldn't he be like Her?
and *me*
if I had such a man
would *I* Still be a Woman?
No most certainly not
SO what was I to do?

*   *   *

And so
should I Do IT or SHOULDN'T I do it
with this Really Great Guy
THAT Was the question
To DO IT OR NOT to DO IT?
        Sitting at my desk

the teacher lecturing about the Hundred Years
War
DO it or not Do it?

'Some sauce over your vegetables?' Mother asks
DO it or NOT do it?

Walking along the lake
feeling the first Sun on our faces
Springtime and the sap is rising
Oh Sweet lord The Time for lovers
DO it

In my treasured pages of poetry
I read ONLY of dewy gardens
saucy little birds tight rosebuds
and emboldened breasts
DO it DO it

YET mother says
if you Wait
the reward will come later
Stolen pleasures can bring no Joy
She Repeats it
Patiently kindly Over and over again
with LOVE in her voice
as if imparting Drop by drop
the Precious secret
to a Happy life
How Could I imagine this sweet mother could
be wrong
that Her words might be UNTRUE?
A wicked stepmother
I would have Disobeyed

But mother was kind and gentle
delicate
fragile and I
Felt I should protect her
No NO No NOT do it

Summer came
and autumn
then winter With its FRESH VIRGIN snow
then spring again
do IT or not do IT?

I'm kissing him
he's kissing me
we cuddle together
endlessly Madly
I feel so good
I love being with him
and not just when I'm In his arms
I love being with him All the time
I love him
DO IT DO IT DO IT

Rah rah hip hip hurrah
          Hey hold it Amélie
          Are you celebrating something?
          Can we join in?
OK everyone
Ready? Here we go
Con tutte le pumone E le carde
          Tra la la la la la

           *   *   *

New York
The Big Happleness

We're through with School Adieu family
Goodbye friends
33 Washington Square West a studio apartment
on the 15th floor
                    Bustle and heat rising from the street below
                    Horns and Sirens
                    A windowsill repulsive
                    black with grime
                    We are HERE
This is Real life at Last
                    Streets Teeming People Everywhere
                    all hours of the day and night
                    'So Amazing Look up at the top of the skyscrapers
                    Dizzying
                    You can't even see the sun it's Crazy'

The two of us Starry-eyed
arm in arm trailing the crowds
                    'Let's go to Macy's let's Do
                    the art galleries'
                    Tomorrow we can go to the Met
                    or Central Park And tonight a movie
                    Finishing the evening with a dripping pizza
                    on a Soggy napkin on the sidewalk
                    and digging into Fish On a Greasy tray
                    Coca cola kisses
                    Perfect bliss

And the SUperrMAHket as they say
Now we're talking practical
not like back home with little baskets of strawberries that

empty into your shopping bag
No here it's Plain Solid Square Pre-packed
Even the bread
No more medieval fussing about fresh bread
'Who's going to buy the bread?' 'Remember
to get the bread'
'Pick up the bread on your way home'
Forget all that
Into the freezer with the Bread along
with the I-i-ss-cream
There's nothing better than the I-i-ss-cream here
Any flavor Any time of year
it doesn't end up squashed at the bottom of your basket
Adieu Strawberries Back to the woods with you
and let's hear no more

Hustled and Jostled in the crush
but Free On top of the World and by ourselves
on our Own at last
Why do Five million New Yorkers seem less stifling
than our two little families Together?
                  'Hey shall we go to the beach on Sunday?'

Crawling back to town after the weekend
                  A procession of silent cars
                  left and Right
                  in Front Behind
                  Three lines of lights trailing back
                  in the other direction too
                  Just Him and Me Émile and Amélie
                  in this Huge rented car
                  stuck in the biggest traffic jam in the world
                  Fabulous
                  It's hot and Muggy

night's fallen
The windows are down the Tyres are
sticking to the road
we're tired and damp with sweat
Bliss Absolute bliss
It's a night I want to keep for ever I don't want it to
fade along with all the others
                As if it holds some precious thing
                The same that I've felt Elsewhere before
                in the frost-covered bush at the top of a path
                in the narrow white streets of Mikonos
                in snowflakes
                swirling
                Something real Of Beauty
                ESSENTIAL
                Life itself
                Life to hold on to whatever the cost
                It's THE LIFE I want to live
                though I've no idea WHERE
                I'll find it

Write about it?
Yes, Write
my Heart's Long desire
Write about the Deep darkness of the night
Capture it in words Seize it
don't let it slip away
                Come on old thing you really should get
                started
                you've talked about it Long enough
                Pick up your pen and Get cracking

              *   *   *

Put Jenny back to bed she'll sleep another hour or two in
the morning A hasty wash Drag a comb through my hair
a Couple of phone calls Put a load of washing into the
machine Now Albertine's crying She's awake again

       Right
       obviously I won't be painting Again This
       morning
       I should get myself better organised

a bottle for Albertine Wait for the burp Change the nappy
And the sleepsuit And the sheet

       For super-absorbent nappies these are more
       like super-crap

Now Jenny's awake again
All right We'll go down to the sandpit
Dress Jenny Little undershirt Little sweater Little
Pants Little coat Little shoes Little hat Little gloves
'Me dress OWN me dress OWN mc dress OWN'
AN E TER NIT Y

       Honestly
       That Émile at his Big desk
       It doesn't look as if he cares two hoots about
       us does it?

Dress Albertine
Tiny undershirt Tiny sweater Tiny
pants Tiny coat Tiny bootees Tiny hat Tiny gloves
FORTUNATELY at least this one's not a
ME-Dress-OWN
Into the stroller Try to cram us all into the lift Jenny GO
to the back Stand right in the corner Careful I have to get
the stroller in It'll squash right up against you Don't move
YOU WANT YOUR TRICYCLE? Are you SURE? It's not
easy you know not easy AT ALL oKay But next time tell
me a Little bit sooner Come on then squeeze out of your
corner and Hold the door so the lift doesn't go down Hold

the door tight It's very heavy for a little girl

> That Émile's got it really good behind that
> desk of his
> No doubt called his secretary to bring him
> a coffee
> Careful not to interrupt your precious work
> Émile or it might not look so serious

       *   *   *

> I can see what's happening . . . that Émile's
> dumped me right in it . . . a companion as long
> as things are going well . . . and he deserts me
> as soon as things get tough . . . he's abandoned
> me in this shit . . . he's a traitor that's what he
> is . . . just wait till he gets in tonight I'll tell
> him . . .
> Just because he does the dishes he thinks he's
> the perfect husband . . . it's not when both
> kids are in bed asleep that I need him . . .
> traitor . . . that's exactly what he is . . . a dirty
> rotten traitor . . .

       *   *   *

I've been ambushed Somewhere along the way Though I
have no idea When Or Where
'You do what you want to do' my parents always Told me
and I chose what I wanted
So why is it ME that's stuck in the house? looking after
kids the Whole day Washing Cooking
for That I didn't need university They should have
FORCED me into a School for Housewives It would've
been less hypocritical I'd never have picked up any notions

about being LIBERATED
I'd never have been so Naïvely trapped

    *   *   *

Oh dear oh dear It's not going to happen
NOT today anyway No writing or painting
It's Certainly Not going to happen today
    Well I might just as well put my paints away
    they'll be awake again soon
    It makes me want to Weep when I think what
    Could have been
    I could Weep
    Oh dear What's wrong with me
    crying like this in the Middle of the day?

    *   *   *

'What's that? what's that Big parcel?'
'That My dear is a SUITCASE'
'You bought a SUITCASE? we've Already got at least six
Isn't That Enough?'
'No I want one of MY OWN
MY VERY OWN'
'But we've Always packed together We've always SHARED
a suitcase'
'Exactly and THAT'S precisely what I don't want
anymore'
'Why not?
what's wrong with our old big brown suitcase The one we
could both put our things in?'
'Well First of all you've NEVER let me pack My things
my way
I have never do you hear NEVER been able to pack even

the slightest pair of socks without you moving them'
'You're off on your exaggerations again'
'Oh No I'm Not exaggerating and you know full well that
I'm not Neither do I want to spend my whole life packing
my case with you looking over my shoulder saying Amélie
Will you never learn how to pack a case properly I've told
you a hundred times to fill the gaps with the little things
Don't put shoes on Top
I've had it
UP TO HERE don't you see?
Up to here with all this Sharing
OUR suitcase OUR car OUR bedroom and just because
we SHARE them
I have to Bend to the wishes of MR Difficult
We say We're going to pack our case
but WE ALWAYS pack OUR
the way YOU want Well I've had enough
I'm twenty-nine years old and *I* want to pack *MY* case *MY*
way and if That's how I like it I'll put my ski boots ON
TOP of my shirts So there'
'Here comes the Women's Lib again'
'Call it What you like and See if I care'
'How kind And if you'll be packing your Liberation too
you'd better buy ten suitcases you'll be needing them all'
'Go to hell'

Epilogue

I don't understand
I just don't Understand how it's happened
What Went wrong?
How on earth did it come to this?
When I think
When I think back . . . you remember . . . I met him . . . I

don't exactly remember Where I met him the first time . . .
one day we danced together . . . those beautiful brown
eyes . . . so gentle when he looked at me . . . he . . .

Translated from the French by ChrisTina Anderes

Jimmy M. Ly

Jimmy M. Ly was born in Pape'ete in 1941 and is of Chinese Hakka descent. Time spent in France to pursue his studies brought home to him the importance of knowing more about his ancestry. He is the author of several books exploring these issues: *Bonbon sœurette et pai coco* (1996), *Hakka en Polynésie* (1997), *Adieu l'étang aux chevrettes* (2003), and *Histoires de feu, de flamme et de femmes* (2006), from which this story is taken.

My Cousin Pouen and the Tyson of Fighting Cocks

He was on his way to his mate Terii's place when he first saw it. A skinny little bird with grey feathers and a sickly look about it. A fellow-sufferer you might say, because although Pouen was a young man he'd been suffering from arthritis for some time. But this cousin of mine, a real island Chinaman, who looked like a work-worn coolie from the Big Plantation, larger than life, caught a glint of something in the eye of this miserable chook, a murderous gleam, the trademark of all real fighters and merciless predators. This didn't escape my cousin's unerring attention, even if the bird in fact completely ignored him. It was love at first sight for Pouen, and by dint of much begging and pleading he managed to persuade the owner to sell him the object of his desires.

He had always been crazy about raising fighting cocks. How did he fall so hard for this one in particular? Even he didn't really know. He told me that he had always been an admirer of these proudly strutting, noble birds, as groomed for combat as those sleek racing cars back when red Ferraris and Maseratis were driven by the legendary Argentine Fangio or the Italian Ascari.

In those days after the war, entertainment in the district was as rare as fishing a salmon from the Teahupoo pass. And so getting together with a few mates who shared a passion for organising cockfights had become the main activity on Sundays after mass or the compulsory outing to church. Since they didn't have a lot of money, they were reliant on the same birds and the same minimal resources to carry out their plans.

The bouts normally took place in someone's garden, big enough and shady enough to serve as a gallodrome: this overly learned word referred to the ring in which our boxing chooks would face off, featherweight class of course. And so their Sundays came and went, to the rhythm of victories and defeats, costing them nothing except a smile of triumph or the disappointment of defeat.

But Pouen was ambitious well beyond the limits of these improvised amateur jousts. It was still his dream to own an outstanding champion. A fighting cock as unbeatable as the great American heavyweight boxers, like his idols Joe Louis or Jersey Joe Walcott. He wanted to raise his noble fighter himself, train it himself—hatch it out in secret, you might say—then present it as an unknown in the town.

He wanted to give the professional breeders the surprise of the century. With his unknown outsider he would be able to confront and defy the capital's grand champions, including the ones from Uturoa on the island of Raiatea whose mythical exploits he had heard about in the market in Pape'ete. And the opportunity came along when his father, who owned a grocery store in the district where they lived, way down south on the peninsula, decided to sell up and try his luck in the big city.

The whole family had to move into a ramshackle old house across from Vienot School. It had a big yard where the hens could frolic to their hearts' content, including the skinny little chook that was the object of all my cousin's love and affection. Shortly after this move, with time on his hands, Pouen started hanging out at the well-known ring in the suburb of Titioro where nearly all the Sunday afternoon cockfights of the 1950s took place.

Who would have guessed back then that a decade later a famous general passing through could set off, on this island and in the Tuamotus, a series of events so cataclysmic that they would alter people's destiny for ever? But that, as Rudyard Kipling so rightly says, is another story, nothing to do with the cocks, unless you take into account that a rooster is the tricolour emblem of French patriotism, and that the whole issue was just as explosive as a cockfight.

The ring in Titioro was on the Fautaua road, just past a bend at the top of a small rise, and it opened off a big yard where there was usually a gathering of Tahitian spectators along with a large number of Chinese. Most of them were dressed in shorts and shirts, some of them were unusually vocal, others much more discreet and even silent, to the point that they didn't say a word even during the fights. Perhaps their enigmatic silence was proportionate to the amount of money they had bet?

With their typically Asian inscrutable expressions, they would shuffle with their equally typically Asian slowness around the cackling combatants, weighing up their chances of future victories. And yet they all had that same sharp and watchful look, the keen eye of the professional gambler, judging and measuring in a single piercing glance the physical abilities and especially the fighting spirit of the cocks on display.

How did they manage to look beyond the triumphant crowing (on the boastful side before a match and therefore often misleading), beyond the slimmed down but not skinny physiques, toned and athletic, almost soldierly, to pick the certain winner? These fluffy gladiators all had the same crested head. Like multiple identical twins, they all had the same bunched and powerful muscles defining their plucked and naked haunches. From the red, almost claret colour of their skin, you could tell how many long hours had been devoted to loving massages with a magic Chinese concoction mixed with tincture of arnica and Mercurochrome. Hardly surprising that at first sight they should all look like potential winners!

This visit to the champions' enclosure, so to speak, was almost compulsory, indispensable, because it wouldn't do for the spectators to be confused over which cock was which when they were about to bet crazy amounts of money: a week's or a month's pay, depending on their means. Should we believe that amongst all this multi-coloured crowd, the so-called ancestral vice of gambling was a part of their genetic inheritance?

Bets were very often placed along a well-defined ethnic line, with Chinese owners in competition and intense rivalry with Tahitians and half-bloods. But that happened in other sports too: for example, a soccer match between the Sam Min and Central (Protestant) clubs always attracted a bigger crowd in Fautaua than one between the Chinese team and the Excelsior (Catholic) club. It was definitely worth the trip just to see Central's centre-forward Napoléon Spitz in all his exasperated frustration, livid with rage against the hermetic Chinese defence.

Win or lose, it wasn't unusual for the birds' owners to lash out at their rivals with sarcastic comments and jeers, unleashing their nervousness before the fight or their relief after they won. And it happened occasionally that racist invective led to quickly suppressed scuffles, whenever there were arguments about the outcome.

I went with Pouen only once, my first ever visit to these meetings where, being thought too young, I wasn't welcome. But the little I saw then filled me with admiration for the splendid creatures on display. You could almost compare them to pedigree pure breeds, they were so beautiful, with their gorgeous multicoloured plumage. They looked like haughty nobles posturing arrogantly and disdainfully. Their aristocratic bearing reminded me of the elegance of English ships on the Tea Route, all slender prows and billowing sails, so graceful that they had become legends of sailing history. When they left Canton, the race was on to see who could make it to Portsmouth in the shortest time, carrying their cargoes of tea, Dragon's Well or Oolong, from the city of Hangzhou. I knew about this magnificent race from China to England via the Indies from a book I had been given for my ceremonial eleventh birthday. Every night I dreamed about the epic journeys of these sea racers, on which fantastic sums of money were bet in London and Hong Kong. Apparently the gambling vice was just as hereditary in the Far East.

On this particular Sunday, proceeding with great care, my cousin had brought his protégé along. There had been months of preparation, a special diet and the appropriate massage regimen. Pouen had told me that what he most liked was his rooster's murderous glare, quite enough in itself to floor his adversaries. Calmly, he followed the other bird owners through the weigh-in and waited patiently for his competitor to be introduced, because today he was the challenger. Meanwhile there were other fights taking place around the ring, which was seething with excited and passionate spectators.

When their turn came, Pouen and the owner of the other rooster went towards the arena. To my novice's eyes, the enemy cock looked just as beautiful and honed for the fight as Pouen's, and I was very afraid of the outcome.

According to the rules on display, which I never fully understood, our adversary was supposed to be more or less the same age and weight as my cousin's bird, so the fight would be even. Meanwhile, the stakes were agreed on between the two owners. These fights weren't just about the glory. The owners also authorised outside bets from their supporters and others, thereby raising the general level of interest. But the real gamblers were already particularly curious about the chances of this outsider Pouen had brought along.

Suddenly, like a wave breaking on the beach, I saw everyone surging towards the arena. I hurried to follow in their wake. The fight was about to begin. Some of the spectators had seats, others just stood there, commenting in loud voices and weighing up the respective chances of the combatants. Listening to them, I sensed that the bettors didn't think much of Pouen. For a few moments the roosters' owners eyed one another, then started to excite the birds by thrusting them towards each other. Then the cocks were finally let loose, practically thrown into the arena. And the battle began, with wracking, Homeric suspense.

It was like Hector and Patrocles, the two most appealing

warriors of the Trojan War, or Sugar Ray Robinson and
Jake La Motta, two American boxers as graceful as big
cats, going head to head to the death, easing off from time
to time only to go at each other even harder. But on this
Sunday, the gods of Olympus or of the noble art didn't come
down to earth to intervene on behalf of the favourite, even
if they might have had a preference for the handsomer and
the more experienced. Maybe that's why the spirit of the
contest changed.

As I said, I'd never seen a cockfight before, but this one
with my cousin's young hopeful gave me a taste for other
combats, an enthusiasm I would later satisfy in French
rugby circles. What a magnificent sight it was, these
creatures leaping at each other in a furious duel, clashing
head on, jumping in spectacular fashion, shockingly swift
and aggressive, and inflicting bloody and sometimes fatal
wounds.

After a few minutes, despite the scrawnier look of Pouen's
rooster, it was obvious that it had the advantage. Its opponent
was making a valiant effort, but was overwhelmed by the
vicious blows of my cousin's bird. At first it had matched
peck for peck and leap for leap, raking its opponent with
raised spurs, but now its head was sinking lower and it
was less steady on its feet. Instead of keeping pace, it was
taking longer and longer to respond, returning only one
blow for every two received. A strange kind of shudder
ran through the spectators around the arena, as they
realised the predictions were being overturned. You could
hear premonitory whisperings of an imminent end to the
fight.

After a number of spectacular rounds, Pouen's rooster's
opponent was exhausted and giddy from so many furious
blows, about to give up. You could see this in its glazed
and staring eyes, but its owner wasn't ready to just give

up. He didn't want to throw in the towel, and in one last effort, was forcing the poor creature to carry on. Even though it was hardly moving any more, he gathered it into his arms. In a gesture at once magnificent and atrocious, he took the bloody crested head in his open jaws, a weird mouth-to-mouth, as if to blow a last breath of redeeming life into his rooster.

Horrified, I could see from the man's expression that he was distressed by the knowledge that defeat was unavoidable. But he clung to his belief, and put his bird back into the arena. In vain. The bird's eyes were sunken with exhaustion. It was taking more blows than before and returning only one for every ten. It was obvious it couldn't go on, and capitulating, it suddenly took to its heels and fled, accompanied by shouts of derision and disappointment from the bettors, and the victory call of its opponent. Against all expectations, my cousin's formerly scrawny chick had won, but everyone who had bet on the favourite lost a great deal of money.

The same wave, only flowing the opposite way this time, and the arena was suddenly empty. Discreet consultations were held a little way off. 'It's the payout,' my cousin told me, as proud as a peacock. A lot of banknotes must have changed hands, because Pouen's rooster wasn't yet highly ranked. Stroking the cock's head and smiling broadly, he said 'This one's a keeper,' while the winner crowed a victory call that must surely have been heard throughout the valley of Fautaua.

We left together, Pouen and I, with him carefully holding his very profitable champion, and me on my bicycle trying to think of an explanation for my parents who were probably worrying about where I had spent my afternoon. There was no way I was going to explain how I had happened to find myself in such a depraved place. Monseigneur hadn't baptised me for nothing.

I went away to France, returning several years later for the holidays. When I saw my cousin again, I asked for news of his champion. He confided sadly that it had died from the effects of its last fight, which it had won. Despite my cousin's best care, its overtired heart had given up the ghost. He had buried it in the yard of the family home, without fanfare or ceremony. His heart had ached that day, because this was no ordinary rooster he had lost. He would forever cherish the memory of its extraordinary feats.

He told me that after that first fight I had witnessed, the bird had been in great demand. Everyone wanted to beat it. It remained undefeated against thirteen opponents. Its outstanding reputation as a fighter was such that cock owners came to challenge it from every district, even from the other islands, and sometimes even with weight handicaps. But his champion always emerged victorious, because it had such a big heart. My cousin said this was definitely the secret of its phenomenal endurance and what had made it outlast all the others in the arena.

A nostalgic Pouen told me he would never see the likes of that cock again, with that threatening look in its eye, a serial chicken killer whose murderous glare alone was enough to bring down each and every adversary. Pouen no longer goes to the cockfight arenas, with their very special atmosphere. But he doesn't miss this since his unbeaten champion died and things will never be the same again. Pouen's passion died forever with his rooster.

Author's note:
Any resemblance to persons living or dead is obviously purely coincidental.

The American boxer, Mike Tyson, was a little-liked champion heavyweight boxer in the 1990s, well known for his swift and cruel knockouts. But Tyson is also an American brand of frozen chicken, probably fed American vitamins, possibly hormones, as its chicken pieces are of impressive dimensions, muscled like bodybuilders. Hardly surprising therefore that this chicken has become a popular, very affordable product; no doubt this is why Polynesians are so partial to it.

Translated from the French by Jean Anderson

Johnny Gavlovski

Born in Caracas, Venezuela, Johnny Gavlovski is a writer, clinical psychologist and psychoanalyst—he is a member of the World Association of Psychoanalysis and the manager of the editorial collection 'Mundo Psicoanalitico'. Johnny has written and produced numerous plays, and was winner of the Municipal Award in Theatre (1987 and 2000) and in Film (1989). He is the author of the novel *Cuerpo de Ambar* (Alfadil, 1989), and a collection of short stories, *Ana, recuerdos de La Casa Verde y otros relatos* (Pomaire, 1994), from which this story is taken.

Antonio by Sundown

From the courtyard of the Church. And there's Antonio, and he looks, out over the peaks, over the peak of Buena Vista, over Santa Ana, over Moruy.

From the courtyard of the Church, Antonio dreams: beyond the only hill of the peninsula lies the sea.

From the courtyard, Antonio looks. Tired of playing, he looks; with his eyes of earth, his look of dust, dust of the road, dust of time, dust of words turned into dust from so much road.

From the courtyard of the Church, he dreams.

In the courtyard, he walks. With his shoes of earth, trousers of air and shirt of clouds. He walks on the sharp stone. He walks on the dust.

'They won't see me any more,' Antonio says to himself. And he runs.

'I won't eat any more.' He shuts his mouth.

'I won't talk to them any more.' And he shuts his eyes, and covers them with his dirty hands, and the tears slip away through his fingers, and he dries them quickly because men don't cry and the children in the Plaza are going to make fun of him, and . . .

The tears slide and leave a damp imprint in the dust. Little tracks on his cheeks.

'They won't see me any more,' Antonio says to himself. And he's angry, and he sticks his tongue out just a little bit, because the tears are nice and salty . . .

'I won't eat any more.' And he shuts his eyes.

'They won't see me any more.' And he runs.

With so many goats in the pen they had no reason to kill Crispín. But they did kill him.

Crispín was nicely painted: with the white of the days, with the black of the nights. While the other goats left the pen to return only at night, Crispín would stay back, and accompany him to the Plaza; and if the children became annoying, they would leave together, go deep into the bush, Crispín and him, him and Crispín, as friends, as pets, as inseparable mates, brotherhood of dust. And it's so windy . . .

Crispín was nicely painted: with the white of the days, with the black of the nights.

And in the bush they played in search of cactus. How Crispín knew where to find them! Then rejoice, then pull them out, then . . . 'Beee.' 'Beee.' 'Stop with the noise, I'll give you some now.'

Antonio bites the cactus fruit. Crispín watches him. Antonio offers him the wounded pulp. Crispín licks it.

Friends, pets, inseparable mates . . .

> The wind
> lifts a cloud of dust
> on the roads.

'Beee . . .' 'Beee . . .' 'Now what's the matter with you, crazy goat?' Crispín runs. Antonio bites the fruit. Antonio chases him. 'Wait for me, Crispín, wait for me.' 'Beee . . . , beee . . .' 'La, la, tralala . . .' 'Beee . . . , beee . . .' The wind lifts the dust. 'Crispín, wait for me.' And the dust is like clouds, but it doesn't rain. It's been so long since it rained. 'Beee . . . , beee . . .' 'Crispín, you crazy goat.'

The sun is like a fireball.
One of his fathers once brought him one. He said: 'Like a red sun.' Mother laughed. One of his fathers said to him: 'Go play outside!' Mother laughed. And playing, and playing, the sun fell on a large cactus. And he called out: 'Mum!' Door of the house shut. 'Mum!' Windows shut.
To discover that the sun is not made of fire. The sun is a red piece of rubber hanging from a cactus.

'What do you want from the cactus, Crispín?' 'Beee . . .' 'I know what you want.' He pulls out his small pocket knife, like a small secret, like a treasure, a memento stolen from one of his last fathers. 'I know what you want.' Steel blade over the tender tip. 'And now I'll cut it for you like this so you can eat the inside.' And the shy drops slide down the steel. 'Get your tongue off or you'll get cut.' 'Beee . . . , beee . . .'

And in the bush they played in search of cactus. And one day they surprised a tropical mockingbird, pecking on a cactus fruit. 'Hey, hey, hey.' 'Beee . . .' And the mockingbird flew away. And he looked at them from above, at them, down there, on the earth, on the dust.

The mockingbird flew away.

Someone warned him about the danger.

'Beee . . .'

With so many goats in the pen they had no reason to kill Crispín. But they did kill him.

He found him that day at noon. He told him nothing. The wind that never comes took away the greetings, the sounds, the gestures. The wind that never comes left him only a wave of heat.

And he was seven years and a few months older than Crispín.

Crispín was nicely painted: with the white of the days, with the black of the nights, with the red of the blood.

'Why did you kill him?'

'Antonio, come and eat.'

'Pick up the droppings.'

'Why did you kill him?'

Adelmo does not reply.

'He was mine.'

Adelmo makes the same father-face that he has seen on all his other fathers.

'Why did you kill him?'

'I told you to pick up the droppings.'

'He was mine!'

'Pick up the droppings, I said.'

Antonio looks and doesn't say.

Adelmo says and doesn't look.

'As if he were your father,' said Mother.

Antonio doesn't know where fathers come from. Adelmo says that he's from Mérida, that this is like hell, that he doesn't know what he's doing here. Adelmo says he had his own house near Apartaderos, but he doesn't know where that is. Antonio calls him 'Father', and Adelmo says to him 'Shut up!' and he shuts up. Mother says to him: 'Ask him for a blessing,' and he does it, quietly, but he does it, and Mother says: 'Go on, spoiled brat. Just like his father.' But he is not like Adelmo. Antonio calls him 'Father,' and knows only that fathers appear one day (like the rain), make it so that Mother is expecting a baby, make Mother laugh (because at night, when there are fathers, she laughs); they also make Mother cry, because he has seen her in the mornings, 'It's nothing, son.' They give orders, hit hard, and then they leave, and Mother gets angry, and they hide together, behind the window.

'Goodbye Father!'

'Shut your mouth, boy!'—says Mother, scared.

And they watch them disappear, far away, in the distance.

'Why are you crying, Mother?'

Very far away.

Like the dust.

'I told you to stick the droppings in the sacks. Be good for something. Earn your keep.'

'My little goat!'

'The droppings!'

'Mum, look at Crispín . . . Mum! . . . Mum! . . .'

'You want your goat, right? You want your goat? . . .'—Adelmo lifts the animal by the legs, body that swings to and fro before the eyes, blood that strikes, that sprinkles, 'Ask him for a blessing', and he's not white and black anymore . . . 'beee . . . , beee . . .' Now he's red and mute and blind and he was seven years and a few months older than Crispín. 'You want your goat, right?'; and Crispín won't be searching any more for cactus fruit, or telling tales to the tropical mockingbird . . . 'You want your goat, right? Woman, go get some coconuts 'cause today we're having goat for lunch. Where are you going, Antonio? Can't you hear me? I'm talking to you! Antonio, get back here and pick up the droppings . . .'

'They won't see me any more,' Antonio says to himself. And he runs.

'Nobody loves us, Crispín, nobody.'

'They won't see me any more.'

'I won't eat any more.' And he shuts his eyes, and covers them with his dirty hands, and the tears escape through his fingers, and he dries them quickly because men don't cry and the children of the Plaza will make fun of him and . . .

'They won't see me any more.'

'I won't eat any more.'

Antonio arrives at the Plaza, but the children are not in the Plaza.

Antonio walks slowly.

Antonio arrives at the courtyard of the Church.

'Antonio, come and play!'

Antonio runs.

Antonio does not want to listen. He runs to the courtyard at the back.

Antonio wants to be alone.

To be so . . .

Antonio leans against the discoloured wall. He cries.

'Once upon a time . . .'

He cries.

'Beee . . .'

He leans his face against the stone. But the stone is cold.

Then Antonio remembers: the old priest is inside the stone. And fear makes the tears stop. The feet back off and the eyes can't stop staring. Beside himself, he's unaware that his knees are bending, kneeling on the dry earth. Antonio stares at the stone, and in his imagination he removes the dust, and goes through the wall.

Shut your eyes.

Fear puts a stop to everything.

Sometimes also memory.

Silence for the memories of seven years and a few months.

Last night he heard the bells, but nobody believes him.

Last night he looked out the window. The bell tower was lit up. He saw it. He tells everyone the story, but nobody believes him. And he tells it, and his mother crosses herself: 'Shut your mouth, boy! Smarten up.' And one day he told it to the new-father-priest, and the new-father-priest said to him: 'Don't believe that nonsense.' But he knows it's true. He also knows that grownups tell lies. He heard the bells ring and saw the tower lit up. He knows it: the old priest showed up last night.

He can imagine his spirit, sitting before the crumbling organ to play the mass. The priest came (as he does each night that he comes), with his priest's cassock, ironed to perfection, and he sits on the bench 'Do-re-mi. Do-re-mi.'

He knows it's true. He knows many things that the old-father-priest taught him, because one day Mother left, a long time ago, when she suddenly got very fat; a long time ago, when he was little, and she said to him: 'I'm going to Caracas, my son.' 'Where is that, Mum?' 'One day I'll take you, Caracas is very far away so you'll stay with the priest, and I'll be back, my son, I swear I'll be back.'

And Mother took him to the Plaza, and the house was

beautiful, and it was white, and it had wooden bars on the windows . . . 'Will you be an altar-boy?' And he said yes because Mother told him that you must always say yes to grownups.

Then Mother left. Time went by and he grew up, so much that he could already reach the doorknob with no effort. Then Mother returned, and hugged him:

'I'll never leave you again.'

'What about the little brother you told me was coming?'

'What are you talking about, son?'

And Antonio has heard many things in his life.

And Antonio knows many things. He knows about the nuns and the bus. He knows there was an accident. And there were nuns, bus, accident, the white house, the wooden bars, the church at the front, and he was little.

He heard it so long ago. So many things happen here!

Last night he heard the bells.

Last night he looked out the window.

Last night the bell tower was lit up. And that's been happening for a long time now, not only during holy festivities. That's been happening for a long time now, and so much has happened since they died.

And the ghost of the priest plays the mass 'Do-re-mi', and the nuns go up to the tower.

Everybody tells the story and Mother crosses herself.

The nuns, the bells: 'DONG—DONG—DONG.'

People talk about it but when he tells it, nobody believes him. 'Shut your mouth, boy. Smarten up.'

Why are grownups like that?

Kneeling on the stone, Antonio stares. He stares at the cold stone.

Antonio knows many things (he has heard many things in his life).

And Antonio hears a noise next to him, and he gets scared, a black shadow, 'last night the tower was lit', and he stands up, and he runs, and . . .

A little black dog is looking at him.

'Woof . . . woof . . .'

'You scared me, little friend.'

Dog that runs, puppy that jumps, and stands on his skinny hind legs, and Antonio takes the other two extended towards him.

'A little race?'

Antonio runs toward the ruins, those of the old houses, those of the nice chimneys.

Antonio runs. 'Bet you can't catch me.' And the dog bites his heels, and Antonio says: 'Hi there, little friend . . . Another race?' And he runs. And 'Woof, woof . . .'

                                        'Beee . . .'

The boy stops. His eyes fill with tears.

Nobody must know. Men don't cry. The children in the Plaza can see him.

'Poor little guy.'

'Woof.'

'Where did you come from?'

Antonio strokes the black head, and also the black back. Hair can be so black under dust . . .

'Go home . . .'

                                'Beee . . . Beee . . .'

'Do what I say! Go home! . . . to your mother . . .'

And Antonio scares him away. And the dog wags its tail. And Antonio shouts at it. And the dog barks. And Antonio runs and the dog jumps, and bites his heels.

'If you don't go away the priest will come for you at

night and pull your ears . . .'

'Woof . . .'—and the puppy sticks out its tongue, and looks at him. Sparkling little eyes.

'You don't have a home, do you?'

A gust of wind and a minute of silence.

Antonio leans against the cold stone.

'Come here.'—And the puppy comes and leans its head on his lap. They look at each other. 'Are you hungry? . . .'

'I won't eat any more.'

'They won't see me any more.'

Asleep.

And the afternoon goes by. Little by little, but it goes by.

'The Church is very old, Antonio. So old . . .'

'Twenty years, Father-priest?'

And he knew how to count up to twenty.

'No, my son, many, many, many more . . .'

'More than twenty, Father-priest?'

'Don't call me that, boy.'

'Sorry, Father . . . More than twenty, Father-prie . . . Father?'

'More than twenty, Antonio,' he concedes patiently.

Father-priest knows so many things. Such lovely stories.

'. . . because the Indians were the first to live here.'

'Why, Father?'

'Because the Lord so arranged it.'

'Why, Father?'

'Because the Lord . . . You ask too many questions, boy!'

And the Indians built the Church a long time ago; long before the father-priest was born. And at that time there were some bad men called pirates and they used to wear a piece of black cloth over their eyes . . .

'And why did the pirates wear . . . ?'

'Let me finish telling you the story, Antonio,' the priest would say, half-statement, half-complaint. 'The Indians prayed because they were good and they were building the Church. And when the pirates came, the Indians would close the doors, go up to the tower and defend themselves.'

'Why, Father?'

'Because the pirates were bad, Antonio.'

The priest would sigh.

Antonio wakes up. The puppy sleeps, head on his lap.

'It's all right. We're going to be friends. What's your name?'

And the dog opens his eyes, his black eyes . . . like the pirates!

'Pirate! Hello, Pirate!'

'Woof . . . woof . . .'

'But you're not bad, are you?'

The father-priest told him that the pirates used to hide treasures, that they used to bury lots of silver in holes in the earth, and that nobody had found it because it was very deep inside, and many years have gone by. Dust of time.

And Antonio has a secret: 'Listen Pirate, I have my own secret too. Two feathers of a mockingbird, a little medal of the Archangel Saint Michael ('So he may look after you and protect you, my son'), four bolívares, two reales, and eight medios. We're rich, Pirate!' Antonio moves closer to his drooping ear: 'Listen to me and don't ask questions.' And Antonio tells him about the people in the refineries, about the ones who have beautiful cars; and he tells him that the fathers want to go over there, and the small town is left on its own, and that some of the fathers return on

Sundays because the father-priest says you have to attend mass, and that the ones with the beautiful cars always want to see the Church and if it's closed 'we tell them: go to the house of the priest . . . That one, you see? The white one. And if he's not there, go to the green one as he most probably left the key there. Should I get it for you, sir? So then you run, you understand me? and you come back and give them the key and when they walk inside, you tell them about the other priest, and about the nuns, and you go up with them and stand there so they take a picture of you . . . Like this, look . . . Like this . . .' 'Woooof . . . Woof . . .' 'Stand like this, Pirate.' 'Woof, woof . . .' 'You ask too many questions, Pirate. Like this, boy, like this . . . and then they give you money, and come over so I can show you where to . . .'

'Let go of that dog or you'll get scabies.'

Who is that woman? What if she wants to take Pirate away from him?

Antonio loves Pirate. He can't take him home. 'I haven't got a home, Pirate.' 'Woooof, woof . . .' And Antonio has an idea. He picks up the puppy and hides it behind some dry bushes:

'Stay there.'

Antonio looks at the tower and runs.

The door of the Church is open.

'Pirate, you have a home now. Pirate, in the tower, in the tower . . . Pirate? . . . Pirate? . . . Pirate, where are you? . . . Piiiiirate . . .'

Crispín was nicely painted: with the white of the days, with the black of the nights. When the other goats left the pen to return only at night, Crispín would stay and keep him company . . .

Where are you?

From the courtyard of the Church. And there's Antonio, and he looks, out over the peaks, over the peak of Buena Vista, over Santa Ana, over Moruy.

From the courtyard of the Church, Antonio dreams: beyond the only hill of the peninsula lies the sea. And they have told him: 'The sea is big,' says Mother. 'Imagine if the plains were all water,' says the father-priest. And Mother tells him that when he was little he saw it, because they were happy and had money and sometimes they would go to Adícora with one of his fathers. 'The sea? If you keep on asking, that's where I'm going to drown you,' Adelmo strikes, and he runs and says to himself, 'I won't talk to them any more,' and he shuts his mouth, and he runs, runs, runs . . .

One, two, three stones. And they're hot.

Antonio throws the stones, and the stones reach far away.

Sometimes he thinks that the hill is a huge stone thrown by a giant boy. Isn't it strange that it's the only hill in the peninsula? Some day he's going to climb it. He heard Señora Martínez say that up there you can find old souvenirs from many, many years ago. Souvenirs from oblivion. Some day he'll climb it. When he grows up he'll be a guide and he'll climb to the very top of the peaks, and touch the clouds (because on that day there will be lots of clouds), and . . . and . . .

One, two, three stones. And they're hot. And they leave your hands full of dust. And that hill is a huge stone that a big boy threw.

One, two, three stones. And they're hot.

From the courtyard, Antonio looks. Tired of playing, he looks; with his eyes of earth, with his look of dust, dust of the road, dust of time, dust of the words turned into dust from so much road.

From the courtyard of the Church, he dreams.

In the courtyard of the Church, he walks. With his shoes of earth, trousers of air and shirt of clouds. He walks on the sharp stone. He walks on the dust.

And the afternoon goes by, little by little, but it goes by.

And Antonio entered the Church, and went behind the altar, small room, the colour of dust, table, chair and blackboard.

The small fingers trace the white letters 'A-B-C', and the fingers are covered in fine white dust and the Indians used to paint their faces; it's just that Antonio knows many things, and the father-priest will teach him how to read someday, and it's just that the teacher got sick and never came back, and the school is closed, but the father-priest said he would take charge. And he knows the names of the letters: the first one is 'A', 'A' for Antonio; and then follows 'B', but Antonio is not written with 'B'; and then comes 'C', and then . . . Then come others that he will learn and . . . The hands are white, white from the white dust of the blackboard and the Indians used to paint their faces, and the small finger slides over the nose . . . 'Here come the pirates.' 'Here come the pirates.'

Antonio runs towards the main entrance. 'The pirates, the pirates . . .' To the right, through the hole down low in the wall, up the stairwell to the bell tower. And he goes in, and it's dark, and he climbs 'lift your feet more', 'It's just that the steps are too high, Father', and as you climb there is more light, and more, and more, and more light. Walls of stone, white and brown, and the steps are also made of stone, of spiralling stone!

And the Indian climbs the stairs, and stands before the window, small on the outside, so wide on the inside, as if it had been built inside out. And the Indian looks out the window and he gets down 'so they won't see him', and he comes to the bell tower, and he hides, and he leans out, and the white fingers are guns. 'Here come the pirates . . . Bang! Bang! . . . Shoot, the pirates are coming . . .' Antonio gets down, and he stands up, and he leans out. 'Thumb, index, and middle finger out. Little finger and ring finger down,' that's what one of the beautiful cars taught him when he showed them around the place. 'Here come the pirates . . . Bang, bang, bang,' DONG, DONG, DOOONG . . . ! The wind moves the bells, the ringing of the wind . . . DONG! 'Last night the tower was lit up' DONG! the nuns! DONG, DONG, DOOONG!, the familiar ring . . . Antonio hears it, above his head, he hears it and he's scared; and faster than Crispín climbing up the hill, he descends the steps. 'Last night the tower was lit up, the nuns stayed here!'

Antonio runs down the steps as fast as he can.

'Mum! Mum! . . .'

And running down the steps it gets dark again. Antonio is scared. Run, run, run . . .

As he comes out of the wall, the darkness of the sacred place. The gate is closed. Antonio looks around, and the fear grows, and it's dark in here, and the gate is closed . . .

'Mum! Muuuum!'

And the fear grows, and it's dark. Antonio hears his own voice. Silence is the reply, and a remote echo of DONG, DONG, DOOONG, and of 'woof, woooof'. 'The pirates were baddies, Antonio.' 'Go get some coconuts 'cause today we're having goat for lunch.' 'Beee, beeeeeee' . . . DONG, DONG, DOOONG . . . ! The tower was illuminated . . . DONG! Illuminated, DONG! Illuminated, DONG,

DONG, DOOONG! closed door and it won't open, it's so heavy . . .

Step back. Three steps back.

Turn around. The hallway is dark between the rows of benches, between the eight massive pillars, under the wooden roof. Universe of three naves, closed. And Antonio walks: one little step, and another, and another, and everything is so dark, so so dark, and he's scared, and his gaze finds him, there, above his head: 'Throw it away, Father, throw it away.' There he is, there he is . . .

Antonio runs to hide under a bench. And then, little by little, he sticks his head out and looks at him; and he looks at him, and he hides again; shrinking, on the dust floor, hiding his head between his knees. He cries. There is the monster. The black dragon, and it seems to him as if it were about to blow flames at him; and Antonio prays to the little man painted at its side: 'Señor Saint George, don't take your eyes off him, don't let go of him Señor Saint George, please, don't let go of him. Kill him, he scares me . . . He scares me! Kill him, please!' And he shuts his eyes even harder. 'They closed the door,' and if he sticks his head between his legs they won't see him. 'And you'll kill him, Señor Saint George, right? Right? . . .' He prefers the face of the little angels over there, or the painting of Saint Ana because she loves them, and this place is named after her, and she's good and she has a book and she reads stories to the little girl there, who is the Virgin when she was little, and Saint Ana is her mum, mum, mum, 'Muuuuum!' . . . The black dragon is over there dragging itself along, DONG! The sound! DONG! The bells, DONG-DONG-DONG! . . . 'Mum! Muuuum . . . !'

'Who's there?'

'Father!'

'Who's that?'

And the father-priest appears above the bench where Antonio is hiding.

'Boy, what are you doing there?'

'The monster, Father.'

'Oh Antonio, it's only a painting. C'mon, come out from under there.'

Antonio comes out. He holds on tightly to the legs of the father-priest and he looks at the dragon.

'What are you doing here, Antonio?'

'I was playing.'

'Your mother is looking for you, my son.'

And to remember, memory of seven years and a few months, and the afternoon has gone by little by little and he . . .

'They killed Crispín, Father.' Antonio cries.

'I know.'

Then the priest lifts him up in his arms, kisses him and strokes his black hair, black under the dust.

'He killed him, Father. Adelmo killed him. He killed Crispín, Father, Crispín, Father, Crispín . . .'

'Adelmo won't be harming anyone else, my son.'

And it's Mum's voice, and Antonio looks up and finds her: 'Mum!' And the priest hands him over: 'Mum!' and she hugs him, and kisses him . . . Kisses the dusty cheeks with her dusty lips . . .

kisses of dust . . .

And Antonio looks at his mother.

'What happened to you, Mum?'

'Nothing, my son, nothing.'

And the little eyes look at the bruised face, the swollen face.

'When did you fall over, Mum?'

'This afternoon, my son.'

'And Adelmo didn't help you?'

'Adelmo is gone. Adelmo is not here any more.'

And Antonio strokes her hair:

'It's better this way, Mum.'

'It's better this way, Antonio.'

'Mum, what are you doing here?'

'I came over to confess, Antonio. I came to confess.'

Night falls. And as it does each day, the Sun hides, below the horizon, over there.

The night that falls, and Antonio looks, towards the hill, over the peaks, over the peak of Buena Vista, over Santa Ana, over Moruy.

'Watch your step, Antonio; you're going to fall.'

And the mother holds his hand.

And they walk on the asphalt, under the light of a street lamp.

'Mum . . .'

'What?'

'Is it true that Adelmo left?'

'Yes, my son.'

'Mum . . .'

'Hmm?'

'Where did Adelmo go?'

'Don't mention that man's name any more.'

And Antonio squeezes her hand.

And along the dirt road, lit up by the weak bulb of a lantern, they walk.

'Mum . . .'

'Yes . . .'

'That man is not coming back, right?'

'No, Antonio; that man is not coming back.'

'When I grow up I'm going to be a guide, Mum.'

'Why do you say that, my son?'

'Because I want to climb the hill, Mum. Señora Martínez says that up there you can find maaany things; old things from maaany years ago.'

'And what do you want old things for, Antonio?'

'To have them, Mum.'

'The things you come up with, boy.'

'You'll see, Mum. When I grow up I'm going to be a guide.'

'No way, my son! You'll be a doctor!'

'Why, Mum?'

'You know a lot of stuff, don't you?'

'And will I have a beautiful car and will we go for rides, Mum?'

'To Caracas . . .'

'No, Mum. To Adícora. Didn't you tell me that's where the sea is?'

'The sea is there . . .'

'Let's go to Adícora, Mum.'

'Stop that now, Antonio.'

And they walk.

Along the dirt road, by the light of the moon, they walk.

'Mum?'

'Hmm?'

'Mum?'

'Tell me, Antonio.'

'And if when I grow up . . . I can be like the father-priest, Mum?'

'Oh, Antonio.'

'So then I get to put away the key to the Church and . . .'

'My son, you're going to be a doctor.'

'And the doctors . . . ?'

'Antonio, let's hurry, it's late.'
'Mum?'
'Walk, Antonio. Walk . . .'

Night falls, as it does each day, when the sun goes
away.
Night falls, little by little, but it falls.
And the wind blows a dust cloud on the roads.
And there is dust,
so much dust . . .

Translated from the Spanish by Desirée Sterental Gezentsvey

Anna Moï

Anna Moï was born in Saigon, Vietnam, in 1955. She studied history in France with the aim of becoming a journalist; however she soon migrated towards fashion and worked as a designer in Paris and Bangkok. She has published two collections of short stories, an essay, and three novels, the first of which, *Riz noir* (Gallimard, 2004), was awarded the Cuneo prize for best debut novel in French. She now lives in Ho Chi Minh City.

This story comes from the short story collection *L'Echo des rizières* (Editions de l'Aube, 2001).

'Ah, je veux vivre dans ce rêve . . .'

Last summer, at the public swimming pool in the city of Condom (Gers), my son dived off the ten metre diving platform. The year before, he had jumped off the boards anchored at three metres and five metres. At the end of the summer, he had leaped from seven and a half metres above water. He then climbed up to the ten metre platform where he stood for quite a while, staring at the water. This year, he stared down again for a long time and I nearly said: 'Hey, it really doesn't matter whether you jump or not.' But I remained silent. Keeping one eye on my book, with the other I watched his every movement. He had been edging towards the tip of the platform and backing away, over and over. Then he stepped forward. Stopped. Glanced at me. I closed my book, looked back silently, raised my thumb, then my forefinger. As my middle finger lifted, he looked right at me to give himself courage, and jumped.

I have never dived from the ten metre platform, not at the age of eleven nor later, maybe because no one counted 'one, two, three'. I dived into thin air guilelessly and without climbing up the ten metre ladder: I sang. I had never sung before. In truth, I wanted to be taught how to breathe: when you breathe properly your chances of overcoming ailments such as fear or pain increase.

People think that war sharpened my anxieties. But the remedy to war-induced angst is simple. You don't have to be breath-trained. Removing yourself from the war is what it takes. I went to France, and the war receded to a far distance. Anxieties dissolved instantly.

The singing teacher said: 'Don't try to sing, breathe.' I breathed very hard, and out came the high C. A door was flung wide open and I was catapulted from a ten metre board into emptiness, terror, amazement, giddiness, freedom.

It's such a strange musical instrument, the voice. Impossible to touch or see. The singing teacher uses imagery. You channel sound 'thinking you are on the ridge of a very steep slope.' You produce the highest notes 'with the note in mind before you vocalise it.' You 'expand the bones of your skull as wide as you can' in order to induce resonation. You sing legato by 'winding up the sound like thread on a bobbin.' And pianissimo is like 'paring the sound down to a thread that you can slip through the eye of a needle.'

My singing teacher's name is Peach Blossom. She is a little lady with big round glasses who lives on the fourth floor of an apartment building—formerly the Saigon School of Dance. Peach Blossom graduated from the Sofia

Conservatory in Bulgaria, where singing is taught according to the rules of the Italian school. Peach Blossom does not speak Bulgarian. This did not prevent her from studying vocal art in Sofia. She has an ear for music, not for foreign languages. She pinpointed one single Bulgarian word, repeated over and over by her teacher: 'nafret', meaning 'forward'. Vocal technique was thus trimmed to the bringing forward of sound.

'Just think that three thousand people are sitting out there, and even the most infinitesimal sound must carry all the way to the back row. I can't tell you exactly where "forward" is. You have to work it out for yourself. I can only tell you if what you are doing is right or not.'

Peach Blossom is a lyric coloratura soprano. Her repertoire includes Juliette's waltz from Gounod's *Romeo and Juliette,* a piece written in a challenging tessitura. The first note is a high B-flat. The war period was, career-wise, a highlight. She sang Juliette in 1968. After her performance of 'Ah, je veux vivre dans ce rêve', the show was stopped and she was ushered back on stage, bowing to her insatiable audience, although the next scene was ready, with sets in place and ballet dancers in position. Her voice was at the height of its power in the year of the Têt offensive.

'The money was not much, but I travelled and I sang. Life was good to me. Others suffered agonies at that time.'

Peach Blossom lives in a decrepit apartment building. Sometimes, on blackout days, complete darkness engulfs four or five metres of the corridor leading to her flat. I feel my way through it until I find the curve of the staircase and climb the four flights. Sometimes, Peach Blossom sends her daughter to the bottom of the stairs with a torch. During the rainy season, the stairs are frequently flooded because the roof leaks. I move carefully through the puddles, wary of their slipperiness. By the fourth floor I am usually breathless, and Peach Blossom hands me a cup of Nhân Trân tea, a Hanoi mixture of herbs and flowers, to help me recover. Her daughter Thu prepares the tea, then withdraws into an adjoining room where she sews. The teapot is always full of the hot beverage waiting for me.

The flat is on the top floor. For an hour or an hour and a half, the duration of the lesson, I stand with my back exposed to the vertical fan. In this position, the back of my neck is cooled while Peach Blossom is sheltered from the draught. The heat never bothers her except for one day, when Viêt-Nam played Thailand. Because of the match, which ended at five in the afternoon (Viêt-Nam lost, 1 to 2), the lesson was postponed for fifteen minutes. On that sole occasion, the ceiling fan was turned on. At all other times, the air is sweltering, and unless I twist my hair up on top of my head, I get no relief from the heat.

All these down-to-earth details are meaningful. Otherwise, the transmission of the intangible art of singing has no markers. You grope about, like in the stairwell, for the switches that open the cavities where sound will surge and soar. You labour to expand your ribs and make room for your lungs. You learn to feel the diaphragm moving. You challenge the soft palate to arch. Over time, you get acquainted with the abdominal cavity, the resonators in the top of the skull, and the circuit in between. When you have almost given up hoping for any further achievement, a door opens, then some time later, another one. There follows a long interval where you want to give up again, but once more, another door is cleared. Finally you manage to understand the impalpable movements of the face bones and the diaphragm muscles that contribute to producing a sound—clear, light, free. None of it seems natural, and yet one day, with no manifest effort, the sound surges out and flies away.

Now that I sing, no tasks impress me as impossible. Vocal victory in the dark corridors has made me invulnerable. I am fearless. I depend on no one but the conductor, to count 'one, two, three . . .'

Translated from the French by Jean Anderson and Anna Moï

Translators

ChrisTina Anderes enjoys discovering new cultures and has a deep interest in languages. Originally from England, she lived for many years in Switzerland (the backdrop to Amélie Plume's earlier novels) and then in Montreal (the setting for Plume's 2006 novel *Chronique de la Côte des Neiges*) where she met Amélie and developed the passion for her works that she now shares through translation.

Jean Anderson is Senior Lecturer in French at Victoria University of Wellington. She discovered her interest in literary translation four years ago, and has since published a number of short pieces and five books, including Janet Frame's *Le Lagon* (co-translation with Nadine Ribault, 2006), Patricia Grace's *Electrique cité* (co-translation with Anne Magnan-Park, 2006), and *Les Yeux volés (Baby no Eyes)* (co-translation with France Grenaudier-Klijn, 2006). She has also translated into English Randell Cottage writer Pierre Furlan's short stories, *Bluebeard's Workshop* (Victoria University Press, 2007) and Tahitian author Chantal Spitz's *Island of Shattered Dreams* (Huia, 2007).

Michael Cronin is Director of the Centre for Translation and Textual Studies at Dublin City University, Ireland. He is the author of *Translating Ireland: Translation, Languages, Identities* (Cork University Press, 1996); *Across the Lines: Travel, Language and Translation* (Cork University Press, 2000); *Translation and Globalization* (Routledge, 2003); *Time Tracks: Scenes from the Irish Everyday* (New Island, 2003); *Irish in the New Century/An Ghaeilge san Aois Nua* (Cois Life, 2005); *Translation and Identity* (Routledge, 2006);

and *The Barrytown Trilogy* (Cork University Press, 2007). He is a founding member and former Chairperson of the Irish Translators and Interpreters' Association.

Stephen Epstein is the Director of the Asian Studies Institute at Victoria University of Wellington in New Zealand, where his research focuses on contemporary Korean literature and society. He has published several pieces of Korean and Indonesian fiction, and won the 1990 Korea Times translation contest in the short story category with Park Wan-suh's 'The Good Luck Ritual'. His co-translation with Kim Mi Young of Yang Gwi-ja's novel *Contradictions* appeared in the Cornell East Asia Series in 2005. He was recently sponsored in Seoul under the Korean Literature Translation Institute's Translator in Residence programme.

Desirée Sterental Gezentsvey is a writer, poet, artist, violinist's wife, mother of three, Jewish, Venezuelan, American Kiwi. After a BA in Modern Languages (Victoria University of Wellington) she completed a Diploma in Creative Writing (Whitireia Polytechnic) and an MA in Creative Writing—Scriptwriting (Victoria University of Wellington). She has had plays and short films produced, and published a bilingual poetry collection, *next time around / la próxima vez* (Steele Roberts, 2006). She describes Gavlovski's story, 'Antonio en la tarde', as a poetic, authentic, and vivid portrayal of rural life in Venezuela.

Nicola Gilmour has been a Lecturer in the Spanish Programme at Victoria University of Wellington since 2001. Her interest in the short story as a genre is a result of her recent development of a course on the Hispanic short story. It is in this context that she discovered Hipólito G.

Navarro's 'Base by Height Divided by Two'. What initially attracted her to it was the narrative's description of a love-hate relationship between twins, and the elusive opacity of Navarro's story which she believed (rightly) would provide an interesting challenge for the translator, as it does for any reader, whether in Spanish or English.

Lisbeth Grønbæk was born in west Jutland in 1961. Although she has spent most of her life in New Zealand she retains strong links to Denmark. She is based in Wellington, has recently been awarded a PhD in French and is currently working in the not-for-profit sector. She chose this short story because the quirky, funny, unpretentious narrative voice that Grønlykke creates has a universal appeal. At the same time, elements of the story are quintessentially Danish. Grønlykke plays on the regional rivalries between Jutland, Copenhagen and Funen and captures the Danes' attachment to their beautiful landscape.

Sarah Hill is a Lecturer in the Italian Programme at Victoria University of Wellington. She has translated a number of texts about aspects of Italian literature, and has a special interest in the work of Gianni Celati. She chose 'Marine Forecast' because it shows Celati's fascination with the ways in which the stories we tell ourselves and each other shape how we see and experience the world.

John Jamieson has an MA in Russian from Victoria University of Wellington and a PhD in French from the University of Otago. He has been a professional translator of non-literary material for twenty-five years, which may well be much too long. He has however retained his interest in literary translation and the problems it raises. His main hobbies are music, running—and of course languages.

Frédéric-Yves Jeannet is a French novelist, critic and interviewer who took up Mexican citizenship in 1987. His first book appeared in 1985, and he has published extensively in France, Belgium and Mexico. His best-known books are *Cyclone* (Castor Astral, 1997), *Charité* (Flammarion, 2000) and *Recouvrance* (Flammarion, 2007). From 2005 to 2007 he taught French literature at Victoria University of Wellington.

Nadine Malfait has an MA in Translation (Dutch/French/English), and an MPhil in French. Originally specialising in the translation of modern art catalogues, she has recently worked in the area of literature and film scripts. Since 1981 she has been a full-time lecturer in the English and Translation and Interpreting Departments at the Lessius Hogeschool, Antwerp.

Richard Millington started working as a translator as an undergraduate in Wellington. After a decade or so of studying, teaching and translating his way through Europe, he has recently taken up a lectureship in German at Victoria University of Wellington, where his courses include a postgraduate translation class.

Rolla Norrish, a trained teacher with a degree in Spanish and an honours degree in French from Victoria University of Wellington, currently works as a translator at the Mexican Embassy in Wellington. She is married with three children.

Sarah Powell teaches French and Francophone literature at Victoria University of Wellington where she is completing her PhD on the short fiction of Claudine Jacques and other New Caledonian writers. She has also translated a number of pieces from French for Radio New Zealand's New Caledonian Season (2007).

Pleasance Purser lives in Wellington. Her interest in Sweden began with a Swedish penfriend. After learning some basic Swedish over the years, she recently decided to learn to read it seriously. The appeal of Åke Smedberg's stories for her lies partly in their setting and, even more, in their understated simplicity, that yet conjures up such sharply focused and evocative pictures. She finds they linger in the memory long after you read them.

Monika Smith studied translation at the Munich Institute for Translators and Interpreters. After more than twenty years of teaching German at Victoria University of Wellington, she is now again working as a freelance translator and interpreter and has also recently translated two children's books for Wellington-based publisher Gecko Press.

Margaret Sutherland is Programme Director for German at Victoria University of Wellington. She has a particular interest in the works of emerging writers in German-speaking countries, and was attracted to Andrea Grill's story for this reason and for its portrayal of the themes of memory and the elderly.

Washima Che Dan is an English teacher and sociolinguist by training, and is currently a lecturer with the Department of English of Universiti Putra Malaysia. Her research interests are in the interconnections between language, ideology and culture, and in the problematics of language and literature, particularly within the contexts of a multilingual nation like Malaysia. She has written on English and Islamic identity, Malayness in Malaysian and Singaporean literature, the politics of language and literature, and gender and sexuality in Malaysian literature.

Sholeh Wolpé is an award-winning poet, literary translator and writer. She is the author of *Sin—Selected Poems of Forugh Farrokhzad* (University of Arkansas Press, 2007), *The Scar Saloon* (Red Hen Press, 2004) and *Rooftops of Tehran* (Red Hen Press, 2008). She is the associate editor of *The Norton Anthology of Modern Literature from the Muslim World* (Norton, 2009) and the co-editor of *Iconoclasts and Visionaries* (Red Hen Press, 2008). Her poems, translations, essays and reviews have appeared in scores of literary journals, periodicals and anthologies worldwide, and have been translated into several languages. Sholeh was born in Iran but spent most of her teen years in the Caribbean and Europe, before moving to the USA.

Yu Young-nan is a freelance translator living in Seoul. She has translated five Korean novels into English, including Park Wan-suh's *The Naked Tree* (Cornell East Asia Series, 1995) and Yom Sang-seop's *Three Generations* (Archipelago Books, 2005). Yu was awarded the prestigious Daesan Literature Prize in 2002 for her translation of *Everlasting Empire* (Eastbridge, 2002). Her co-translation of Han Sung-won's *Father and Son* with Julie Pickering made the 2002 list of Kiriyama Pacific Rim Notable Books.